Where Are the Prophets?

BY THE SAME AUTHOR

Onward Christian Socialist

Terry Wynn MEP

Where Are the Prophets?

Matador
9 De Montfort Mews
Leicester LE1 7FW, UK
Tel: (+44) 116 255 9311 / 9312
Email: books@troubador.co.uk
Web: www.troubador.co.uk/matador

ISBN 10: 1 905886 25 X
ISBN 13: 978-1-905886 25 8

Typeset in 11pt Bembo by Troubador Publishing Ltd, Leicester, UK
Printed in the UK by The Cromwell Press Ltd, Trowbridge, Wilts, UK

Matador is an imprint of Troubador Publishing Ltd

To James David and Amelia Grace,
true gifts from God.

I confess that I have never met a man quite like Terry Wynn. He is a man of deep faith and convictions. Sometimes controversial and provocative, yet transparent, vulnerable, and open about why he feels the way he does. In this book he has deposited a part of his life as a public servant which will be of benefit to readers of many different walks, generations, and cultures.

Bill Hightower
President, Tower Strategies, Inc.

CONTENTS

ACKNOWLEDGEMENTS

There's a whole list of people without whom this book could not have been written. First there are those who willingly agreed to be interviewed, Ulrich Miesel, Tunne Kelam, Maat Laar, Vytautes Landsbergis, Boris Trajkovski, Albert Nolan, Tony Hall, Iain Paisley, Ibby Adia, Louise Ellman and Glenys Kinnock.

Then there are those from whom I have quoted:

Phillip Yancy from *The Bible Jesus Read* and *Where is God When it Hurts*, Richard Coles from *Restoring Faith in Politics*; Graham Dale from *God's Politicians*; Jim Wallis from *The Soul of Politics*; John Ashcroft from *Lessons From a Father to a Son*; Martin Westlake from *Kinnock*; and finally Dennis Healy from *The Time of My Life*. In addition, the correspondence of Paul and Rebecca Petrie for their "Rebecca's Journey" messages.

A special thanks to Cedric Mayson for giving me some better ideas and for the pieces that he wrote, and to Phil Sudworth for some excellent advice.

Last but certainly not least the members of my staff who transcribed recordings into script, Olwyn, Laura and Alexander, but a special thanks to Marilyn who has done the bulk of the work whilst at the same time doing her job as my P.A. and still putting up with all the work my office generates.

FOREWORD

Rt Hon Lord Patten of Barnes CH

No disrespect to Terry Wynn, but he is not the best known politician in Britain.

Yet he is one of the most accomplished parliamentarians I have ever encountered—wise, resourceful and constructive. His role in the European Parliament, most notably as Chair of the Budgets Committee, demonstrated just how much real power can be exercised by leading members of the European Parliament, much more than is available to most national parliamentarians.

The European Parliament is in some respects its own worst enemy. Victim admittedly of the deal done by member states to assuage French grievances over a decade ago to move like a travelling circus between parliamentary buildings in Brussels and Strasbourg, it is further encumbered by the fact that it simply does not take itself sufficiently seriously. Debates have been allowed to turn into a procession of timed speeches, with those who make them rarely taking notice of what others say. Much more important, the Parliament has not encouraged the creation of a real career path for its more able members. So the new President of the Parliament, no doubt a capable man, had never sat in the Parliament before his elevation. A more serious parliament would insist that its principal figures had experience of its operations.

Terry Wynn begins by recounting how this happened in 2004 to his own disadvantage, but characteristically he does so without a hint of bitterness. And this is germane to the main theme of his book—the place that a deep spiritual commitment, in Terry's case Christianity, can play in someone's public life.

For Terry there is no tension between his commitment as a Methodist and as a successful socialist politician. He is not sanctimonious or "preachy". He is not a hypocrite or humbug. There is no intolerant bumptiousness or extremism about him. Terry's career should remind the cynics that politics is not full of careerist chancers. What you get with Terry, is what you see—a man whose ethical sense informs his everyday life and his calling as a Christian.

You won't find the point made better anywhere else than it is by Terry's book. I do not share his politics, though I am a Christian believer like him, albeit from a different church. I learned a lot from this book, and wished after I read it that I had always been as successful as Terry in balancing the pragmatic demands of politics with the ambitions for us all of the New Testament, which raises our sights far above the lives we are normally capable of living.

PROLOGUE

"We can win this, we can win this." The words went excitedly through my mind as Hannes Swoboda, the Austrian candidate, told me he was withdrawing from the contest. The 6th July, 2004, would be the penultimate hurdle to get over before becoming President of the European Parliament. The Slovenian, Borut Pahor, would pull out too, which left a straight vote between Borrell and me. It was going to be a clear choice between North and South and we could do it. The French, Spanish, Portuguese and Greeks versus the rest; the French and Spanish may be the biggest delegations but the new member states and Northern Europe would vote for me.

Swoboda had said in his hustings speech that the President can't be from Iberia since the Portuguese were getting the President of the Commission and the Spanish with Solana would get the Foreign Minister's job. He could have added that there have been two Spanish Presidents of the Parliament in the past three mandates and this would be the third in 15 years if Borrell won. And now Swoboda was withdrawing so his supporters would vote for me.

The hustings had taken place the afternoon before, with Borrell exceeding his allotted ten minutes to speak for fifteen. I thought he was good, especially for someone who hadn't been in the Parliament before. He was a former Spanish Cabinet Minister, quite a big cheese in his own country and was now leader of their delegation in the Socialist group which we were addressing and which was going to vote to decide who would be the Socialist candidate for the President of Parliament.

An agreement had been reached between the Socialists and the centre-right PPE group to deliver the votes for the socialist candidate for President now in July 2004 and then in two and a half years time, when a new President was voted for, the PPE candidate would be elected and the Socialists would then support him or her, a kind of you scratch our backs and we'll scratch yours. So, whilst the vote in the plenary was the final hurdle, this was what counted. Win this and I would be the next President of the European Parliament. The first British Labour Member ever to be so.

When Borrell had finished his speech, next came the Slovenian, the only Socialist elected in his country, a former speaker of their Parliament and not to be taken seriously for this contest. Next came Swoboda. I looked at his notes as he sat next to me; they were non-existent. A few jotted lines, three main points and a plea to vote for him because he came from Austria and would represent the small countries. He was awful. Come the likely event that I went out on the first ballot along with the Slovenian and it was a run-off between Borrell and Swoboda then my vote would be going to the Spaniard.

Then it was my turn. The speech had been well worked on. I'd done the basic outline in Tuscany the week before on holiday then polished it up with Maggie Coulthard's help on the Monday morning. A lot of prayer had gone into this—"Let me not let you down, Lord, if this is what you want me to do, If I don't get it, then let me know how I can serve you." What I was really trying to say was, "Lord, I'm desperate to get this, it's what I really, really want. You've got me this far, over several hurdles already, now get me over this one. This is how I can really serve you, at a time of massive Euro-scepticism especially in the UK, with the success of the UKIP getting 12 seats, I can take them on to help unite the people of Europe." I did add the rider "Of course Lord, if it's not to be, then show me how I can serve you," hoping that this was the thing to say but would be ignored by God.

Whilst Swoboda was speaking, I suddenly became totally relaxed. I was singing to myself a catchy chorus we'd had the day before in church, "I have decided to follow Jesus." It's very repetitive and it kept going on and on. I thought any moment now I'm going to jump on the bench and burst out in song—that really would blow my chances. Then a little silent prayer, to be with me Lord, let me say the right things etc. Then it was my turn.

Wasn't that just brilliant? (The word hubris springs to mind at this point). The bit where I said, "Some in here say they can't vote for me because I'm a Brit ("Yeah!" shouted someone). Now I don't mind people voting against me because they don't like me, or because they think I'm incompetent but when this Group begins to vote against someone because of their nationality then the solidarity which holds this group together will soon begin to disintegrate," brought spontaneous applause; none of the other three had had that in their speeches. I stressed my passion for Europe and outlined the vision I had. It was good stuff. I ended by saying, "With your support and trust, I guarantee that passion and vision will never diminish." Wow, that was V-E-R-Y good. I felt like taking a bow.

Then came the question and answer session and it was obvious that Borrell and I were the only two serious candidates. Once again it went splendidly well. As it finished I went to Borrell and said, "You were very good," thinking, "but not as good as me."

I left the platform with lots of congratulations but also with a contented feeling that whatever the result I knew I had done my best, given a good performance and gained respect, especially from the many new members. It wasn't a feeling of triumph but one that recognised that events were now out of my hands; I couldn't do any more and if I lost then, then....at least God had been with me when I wanted him to be.

★ ★ ★ ★

It had all started earlier in the year when I was trying to figure out where I wanted my career to go. I'd been an MEP for 15 years and had been remarkably successful in the roles that I had had. For the past five years I'd been chairman of the Budgets Committee; there aren't many better positions and to do something with more clout was pretty limited. After 15 years I was ready to look for something else, not to stand in the June 2004 elections and go out on a high. Trouble was, I had no plan or idea of what I wanted to do. Mike Hindley, a former colleague who had left the Parliament five years earlier said he'd spent his last year networking so he could make the right contacts to establish his consultancy when he left. When have I had time to network? The chairman's job is so demanding and also so fulfilling but it gives no time for, what was it—networking?

Then Gary, the Leader of the European Parliamentary Labour Party (EPLP) said that the Socialists would get the Presidency for the first two and a half years of the next Parliament and that's what I should go for. What a good idea.

First thing was to convince the EPLP that it was a good idea; second thing was to beat David, the existing British Labour Vice-President, an MEP for 20 years, a talented guy but as much as I genuinely liked David as a person, he hadn't really done much in the Parliament for years, except that he chaired the plenary well. The European Parliamentary Labour Party consisted of 28 MEPs, several of whom would be leaving after the June elections. But they decided we should make our minds up what positions we were going to go for in the new mandate then they could be reconfirmed by the new EPLP after the elections. At the first discussion I made it clear that I was aiming for the President's job, so did David. At least we had both brought it out into the open.

Before the next meeting, when a vote would be taken, David's estranged wife Margaret had made allegations about his Parliamentary expenses and an investigation began. So come the meeting there were those who said the contest shouldn't take place since David had indicated he wouldn't stand with this investigation still ongoing. The EPLP decided it should go ahead and I made another speech that kicked modesty out of the window. Lots of prayer had gone into it, "If it be your will", etc. and I got the nomination by 20 votes to four with two abstentions and two not present. How humble did I feel. More than that I felt that I was being pushed into the role, like divine guidance. (Who said "Give me a bucket?")

Next task was to let all the heads of the other 14 delegations, from the other 14 countries in the Socialist Group, know and say I was willing to speak to them. The feedback was excellent. The only other serious contender was Renzo Imbeni, an Italian who I got on with very well. But then as the Italians were drawing up their lists of candidates for the elections, Renzo was omitted. He wasn't on, this was going to be a clear run. Go to number 10, tell the politicos there and the civil servants and the Europe Minister, Dennis McShane. It was going to happen, the group has never had a vote on these things, they were carved up by the delegations and we had made the running. I'd spoken to Enrique Baron, the President of the Socialist Group and to Martin Schultz, the German leader who was hoping to be (and eventually would be) the next President of the Group. Knowing that the Germans or the British were always the largest delegations, if we supported him then they would support us, i.e. me. His words to me were, "As far as I am concerned, Terry, you are the next President of Parliament." Don't forget Hans Gert Poettering, the leader of the PPE group. All we needed was the elections out of the way.

June 10th, 2004, was the day of the European elections in the UK with the count on the Sunday the 13th when the rest of Europe had voted. Our objective was to hold our four seats in the North West, which we should just about do. I'll do two and a half years as President, resign and Theresa would take my place, she being number five on the list and an automatic successor should any of the other four stop being MEPs.

As the votes came in, I was convinced we had the four seats, that is up to ten minutes before the final votes were in and I realised we only had three. Brian had lost his seat. What an unmitigated disaster and what a loss, my mate Brian. He'd been there 15 years like me, we watched Wigan rugby together, we'd formed the Rugby League Intergroup together, he was a Wiganer through and through like me and he wasn't elected.

The Liberals and UKIP had each taken a seat from Labour and the Tories, this was a bad night. Ralf Walter telephoned me from Germany, the SPD had taken a drubbing. When the dust settled the EPLP had gone from 28 members to 19 and the Germans down from 35 to 23. Five years before there had been 60 (originally 62) Labour members. Thanks to the Labour government's introduction of Proportional Representation for the European elections we had gone from ten out of ten Labour members in the North West in 1999 to three out of nine now.

The elections had thrown up some strange results; the French were now the largest delegation in the group with 31 members, next came the Spanish. This was a whole new ball game; normally the Anglo–German axis dominated, now we had France and Spain in pole positions.

Come the Tuesday after the results, the EPLP reconfirmed my candidature. David stood this time, even thought the enquiry was still ongoing, but it was now or never for him. The vote was twelve for me, six for David with Glenys off to Uganda. "Thanks Lord, if it be your will, I feel like I'm being pushed, but hey, that's another hurdle over."

Come the Wednesday I was off to Tuscany with my family to have a well earned rest after months of campaigning. Gary, as leader of the EPLP, was off to Brussels for the heads of delegations meetings of the Socialist Group.

★ ★ ★ ★

The President of the European Parliament has a private Cabinet of 32 people, which includes advisors, secretarial staff and even the President's driver. I'd asked Michael Shackleton if he would be the Chef de Cabinet, one of the brightest brains in the place, and also a genuinely nice guy. We set about drawing up the list of other members of the team and informally asking people if they would be interested. Others approached me direct, asking if they could work for me—word was getting round fast. The drivers in the car pool were telling everyone it was me and Ronnie had already asked if he could be my driver. There was a lot to ponder during the holiday.

Tuscany, was, as ever, beautiful. La Colombaia, the place we always stayed was welcoming, set in the perfect location to watch the sun set behind San Gimingnano, and the pool was just for us.

The greatest joy I have is spending time with my family and they would all be here for my birthday. Having time with your children, your adult children, is one thing, but having a full week with my two-year-old grandson, James, is something else.

I don't have enough love for the amount I want to give to my family. One of my favourite verses was in a book, *When Iron Gates Yield*, and it's the words of a persecuted Christian written on the wall of a Chinese prison cell:

> "Could I with ink the oceans fill,
> And were the skies of parchment made,
> Were every stalk on earth a quill
> And every man a scribe by trade,
> To write my love of you my God,
> Would drain the oceans dry.
> Nor could the scroll contain the whole,
> Though stretched from sky to sky."

Substitute the word 'God' for 'family' and that's it exactly. It's what politicians need more than anything—when everyone may seem to be against you, what matters is the love and trust of your family. So it couldn't have been better.

The first warning signals were when Gary said the French may ask Swoboda to stand for President. I did a bit of ringing round to various people I know to get a feel of things. Joan Colom, a former colleague, now the head of the Catalan Court of Auditors, gave some good information. Borrell would be looking for something and he thought it would be Chairman of Budgets, my existing, soon to be old, job. One thing's for sure, the Spanish, with a lot of new members, would be reluctant to vote for a Brit. They didn't like Mr Blair's relationship with Aznar, the former Prime Minister. "Yeah, but it's me, Joan, not my Prime Minister who is standing." "I know, Terry, I'm sorry to be the one to tell you, but it's my assessment." He's a wily bird, Joan (pronounced Jo-An, it's Catalan you see).

OK, so that's the French and Spanish against. More phone calls, Gary doing the business. Things beginning to happen.

In April earlier in the year the Party of European Socialists elected a new President. Paoul Nyrup Rasmussen, a former Prime Minister of Denmark, had narrowly beaten Amato, the Italian candidate. I thought Rasmussen the right decision and couldn't understand why the British delegation had supported Amato. I hadn't been a delegate so didn't know what went on, but well done Paoul. My close friend Freddy Blak, a larger than life character who everyone in Denmark knew (normally no-one can name an MEP in the UK, but Freddy is known by all the Danes), had said he would speak to his former Prime Minister to ensure the Danish delegation supported me. I phoned Freddy a couple of times and left that in his capable hands. Others I contacted were supportive but the emergence of Swoboda was giving the small countries a chance to vote for one of their own.

There was also the complication that probably 50% of the Group would be new members and not know me or my track record. The eight Greek socialists were all new, in the old Parliament George Katiforis, their leader, had been very supportive. The five Danes, including Rasmussen, were new and goodness knows how many of the French were new.

Gary's latest stop-press, Borrell is in the running. Hang on a minute, this guy is brand new to the place, does he have the French on his side or are they pushing Swoboda? In the meantime the Constitutional Treaty has been agreed by the heads of government. Tony Blair has done a great job; it's a British Constitution according to the French. "What about the lack of references to Social Europe?" they say. Tony then vetoes the Belgian Prime Minister as the new President of the Commission, because he is too federalist. Chirac then vetoes Chris Patten. The Portuguese PPE Prime Minister, José Durao Barroso, is the chosen one for the Commission top job, with the support of the British government. This hasn't pleased the Portuguese socialists and a lot of the others view him as "too close to Bush and Blair" and too much of a Blairite.

Pasqualina Napolitano publicly states she would support Michel Rocard for President of Parliament. Where the hell has his name come from and does it mean all the Italians will support him? Dennis McShane, the UK Europe Minister, says in a PES meeting he can't understand why the French are not putting Rochard forward. This sows total confusion, especially with Martin Schultz, the leader of the German delegation. "Does the UK government support Terry or not?" I get Doriano to contact Gianni Pittella, my Italian mate (Doriano speaks better Italian than me—well, he is Italian—and Gianni only has broken English).

I speak to Max van den Burg, leader of the seven Dutch members; "Terry, Jan Marinus and I will certainly be voting for you. I can't say what the rest will do." Zita Gurmai, of the Hungarian delegation, who were 100% behind me, "Swoboda has given our delegation a problem. Our leader says since he is a neighbour we should vote for him, but a lot of us are still with you."

Get Goran Farm to keep the Swedes on side. He says there isn't a problem.

Reino Paasilinna says he and his Finnish colleagues will put in a good word for me when the Baltic delegations meet together to decide who to vote for.

The heads of delegations can't do a deal; what are you playing at Gary? Alan Donnelly would have had it sorted by now. But Alan, the biggest wheeler dealer of them all, left four and a half years ago to wheel and deal elsewhere. There's going to be hustings. Never before has the Group done this to decide who its candidate will be. But that's ok, it may scare the Spanish guy off, he's never been in the Parliament before, and I can perform when I have to. Reino had said that it may come down to who performs best on the day. Well, perform I can. "Be with me Lord, let me give my best, if it be your will. Oh, and if its not your will, then let me know what you want me to do to serve you (concentrate on the former if you would Lord)."

★ ★ ★ ★

Sixth of July, 9 am, Martin Schultz announced that Swoboda and the Slovenian had withdrawn. Swoboda makes a speech and in translation I lose the bit where he mentions Borrell. What's he doing giving his support to him? Surely not, he said yesterday we can't have a Spaniard. Surely not.

Cast your votes. I do. I have a coffee, chat to one or two and when they ask for a prediction, I reply, "We can win this on the assumption that we can pick up Swoboda's votes." We resume for the result. Martin Schultz says he has the result. "Lord, let me handle this, let me do it well, be with me."

"And the result is Josep Borrell 117 votes, Terry Wynn 66 votes, therefore I

I applaud of course, he makes a thank you speech, then comes to embrace me and I smile and say "Good luck, do it well," and that's it.

Quick prayer, "Lord help me to handle this"; but then I think, "Why have you brought me so far, why did you let me stand in the elections, so much was banked on this, so many people have been praying for me, so many people knew and were supportive, so much emotional energy has been ploughed into this? But I've learned not to ask why. Accept it, there's no turning back, it's done. Phone Doris, tell the kids, tell Michael and Alfredo, shake hands, take the commiserations gracefully and keep smiling; whatever you do don't show disappointment. "It was the wrong result," says Barbara Weiler, a German member, "How can we have someone as President who has never been in the Parliament before?" I feel like a Dennis Healey figure—the best President the Parliament never had. Gordon Adam, who is about to leave after twenty five years as an MEP, goes back to his office and says to Stuart his assistant, "If in the future you begin to see the EU starting to unravel, then put it down to this date."

One thing I know for sure, I won't be staying in the Parliament; what I need now is an exit strategy. "Guide me as to what you want me to do, Lord." I'd often said, "God puts you where he wants you to be." Well, he didn't want me to be President of the European Parliament, that's for sure. But I did.

★ ★ ★ ★

The analysis of the result was quite revealing. The large margin had shown a big anti-British vote because of Iraq, the Constitution, Social Europe and the Commission President. Hardly Gary's fault, even Alan Donnelly wouldn't have stopped this. Colom's assessment had been correct but it had gone much further than the Spanish. On my reckoning, the Swedes, the Finns, virtually all the new members states, two Danes, three Dutch and only half the Germans voted for me; the rest voted resoundingly against. In elections back home I often say no-one voted for me because my name is Terry Wynn; they voted for me because it said Labour Party candidate after my name. The same theory applied in reverse here.

How had the ball started rolling? Rasmussen owed the Brits no favours according to Helle, one of the outgoing Danes, because of their vote for Amato. He wanted to prove that as President of the Party of European Socialists that he had influence and could fix things. So he did. Not only did he get Borrell to stand but also Swoboda to split my vote, then persuaded Swoboda to stand down and support Borrell. That's politics.

Freddy Black had left 20 messages with Rasmussen; not one was returned, so he went to see him to get him to support me. But it was too late. Even before the elections Rasmussen knew what he was going to do.

In the words of Kenneth Williams in Carry on Cleo: "Infamy infamy, they've all got it in for me."

To be honest, yes I was disappointed, but not devastated. I do genuinely believe God puts you where he wants you to be, so its no use moping about it; it's a matter of accepting it and getting on with things. At least I still had a job, unlike Brian and many other colleagues who weren't re-elected.

In 1994 after the then elections I stood to be leader of the EPLP and was defeated by Wayne David. I walked back to the flat from that meeting absolutely devastated. I was so used to winning I couldn't accept I had been rejected. Yet that defeat was probably the best thing that happened to me. Not being leader let me be general budget rapporteur for a second time; the only person ever to do so and also I became the socialist co-ordinator on Budgets; in American terms that reads Majority Leader on Budgetary Matters. That laid the foundation for being the Chairman of the Budgets Committee. Had I been elected leader none of that would have happened. And what did Wayne get but 61 whinging politicians complaining to him continuously about anything and everything.

Also, when I had finished the hustings that feeling of contentment was real and I knew it was no longer in my hands.

But more than anything I was quickly able to put things in perspective. The time with my family whilst I was doing all the telephoning confirmed my belief of what the important things are in life. As long as I have them, what does it matter what position I hold? But one thing kept continually running through my mind and when people asked how I felt, I gave this reply: "There is a young woman at our church back home called Suzanne, happily married, young family, good job, girl-guide leader. She had been diagnosed with an inoperable tumour behind one of her eyes. Now that is something to worry about, not whether I became President of Parliament or not." And the thought of Suzanne and her problems have helped me overcome, what is after all, a minor set back.

I went to bed on the Tuesday night, seeking guidance from God, trying to be reverent in my prayers. Didn't sleep well, but woke up about 6 am with the words, "Stop feeling sorry for yourself" on my lips. Appreciate the things in life that are good, look at all the blessings that you've had and make the effort to begin the next phase of your career. Start on that book you're always going on about. Right!

So here it is.

ONE

"You can't put things like 'Swoboda was awful', he may read it," Jane, one of my Brussels assistants, had said after reading the first draft of the Prologue.

"Yes I can," was my response, if only to show exactly how I was feeling, to demonstrate the arrogance if nothing else. I'm more concerned with Gary and David being offended, but I wanted to ensure that what was going through my mind was accurately reflected; the hopes and aspirations, the concerns and the rejection.

To write it was a cathartic exercise done almost the day after the vote and hopefully it would set the scene for what follows.

When I first had the idea to write a book I thought it would be good to compile one about Christians in politics. A book to be entitled *Faith in Politics*, or something like that. However, the Christian Socialist Movement have already published one with a similar title *Restoring Faith in Politics* so I would have to think of something else.

The original idea was to get statements, speeches or whatever from people I knew or had contact with. It was easy; get a dozen or more people to do their bit, put it all together and hey presto, we have a book.

I then emailed Cedric Mayson (of whom more later) in South Africa, asking if he could get some details of people like Smangaliso Mkhatshwa, a prominent Priest and Politician and in fact himself and even Madiba (i.e. Mandela) if possible.

Cedric's reply changed everything, however. The ideas he stimulated suddenly suggested a book worth reading. He gave lots of ideas making the point that the story of what faith in politics does to individuals has to be put in the wider context, which looks at the general attitude to both faith and politics that

1

needs to face criticisms and challenges, and should point a way forward not only in theory but from where readers are sitting. It must stir faith that can act politically in the reader's situation.

I was now wondering if it should be in the context of a world, and countries, which are in great need of faith and why a majority of people have lost faith in both religion and politics.

He made me realise that half a dozen people all saying the same was of no use, so some of the interviews could be with right-wing fundamentalists and political criticisms of believers should be included or the way in which religious people have promoted barriers.

He reminded me that the ANC National Executive Committee, with the top brass present, has spent the past three days working on the moral regeneration of South Africa, a deep and wide ethical renewal, analysing why things go wrong, what is wrong with them, and what directions they must take to answer their political and economic challenges and problems in the context of a quest for moral regeneration.

Cedric certainly made me think and swayed my ideas away from the simplistic format I had first envisaged. He also made me think, what do we mean by faith in politics? Is it just politicians with faith and if they do have it, what difference does it make? Why stick with the tried and tested Christians who won't cause too much offence, why not get the John Ashcrofts (the USA Attorney General at the time of writing) and the Ian Paisleys of this world to comment.

Cedric wasn't the only catalyst, Paul Petrie had given me the book *The Bible Jesus Read* by Philip Yancy. I'd read his *What's so Amazing about Grace* and was bowled over by it, this was my kind of Christian writer – he was up there alongside Thomas Cahill for his *Hinges of History* books. In *The Bible Jesus Read*, Yancy, to quote from the dust cover, "admits that, like many Christians, he usually avoided the Old Testament. After all, why bother with writings that can be so baffling, even offensive to the modern mind." He dissects selected books of the Old Testament like Job, Deuteronomy, Psalms and Ecclesiastes, and it was while reading his chapter on Ecclesiastes that the need to do this book gained even more momentum.

Let me give you some idea why. He starts off by saying how he was into Existentialism in the avant-garde world of the 1960s. He asked the searching question "Why am I living?" "What is this circus all about?" "Can one person among five billion make a difference on this planet?" Existentialism, he says, gave a sort of answer by saying there was no answer, that life would go on no matter what you did and that a human being after all is just a time blimp in the billion-year progression of history.

Why should that sort of thing excite me? Because most of the people I work with and a lot I socialise with have that same existential feeling and here was Philip Yancy giving some great counter arguments, but based on Ecclesiastes. Ecclesiastes, the original book on existentialism, the book that begins in the King James version of the Bible with "Vanity of vanities, all is vanity." Or in modern parlance "Meaningless, meaningless, utterly meaningless! Everything is meaningless."

To quote from Philip Yancy, "That key word meaningless appears 35 times.... The issues bothering the author of Ecclesiastes were the same ones that bothered Job, and that bother all fair-minded people today. The rich get richer and the poor poorer, evil people prosper as good ones suffer, tyrants reign, disasters happen, disease spreads, everyone dies and turns to dust. Life is unfair. Nothing makes sense; the whole world seems off-balance and twisted.

"Forget prudence, concludes Ecclesiastes. Eat, drink and seize any fleeting moment of happiness. What else is the point of living? You work hard and someone else gets all the credit. You struggle to be good and bad people trample you. You accumulate money and it goes to spoiled heirs. You seek pleasure and it turns sour.

"Besides, everyone—rich or poor, good or evil—meets the same end: we all die. Death, the ever-present, stalking spectre, contradicts any notion that we are born to be happy. There is only one word to describe this life: meaningless!"

Jean-Paul Sartre, Albert Camus et al. were repeating sentiments of 3,000 years before.

Why should it matter to a book about faith in politics?

Because Ecclesiastes was written in Israel's golden era when things were going really well, not in the days of exile or slavery. And any philosophy gained from my own experiences of people I've met, whether in Eastern Europe or in

South Africa is that in affluent times people forget about God. Let Philip Yancy continue to explain: "It had always seemed odd to me that the modern existentialist philosophy of despair originated in one of the loveliest cities on earth, Paris, during a time of expanding wealth and opportunity. Curiously, I learned, existential despair, whether in the Teacher (of Ecclesiastes) or in Camus, tends to sprout from the soil of excess. Why?"

Then he quotes from *The Message in the Bottle* by Walker Percy who asks: "Why do more people commit suicide in San Francisco, the most beautiful city in America than in any other city?" (In Europe the suicide capital is Salzburg, Austria.)

"Why was it that Jean-Paul Sartre, sitting in a French café writing *Nausea*, which is about the absurdity of human existence and the nausea of life in the 20th Century—why was he the happiest man in France at the time?"

Philip Yancy says that Percy's explanation is that despair arises out of circumstances of plenty rather than deprivation. He goes on, "Indeed, I did not find alienation and despair in the grim, three-volume *Gulag Archipelago* by Solzhenitsyn; I found rage, a passion for justice and a defiant will to survive. As Viktor Frankl explains in *Man's Search for Meaning*, the victims of the concentration camps, he among them, did not dare succumb to meaninglessness, for only an enduring faith in meaning kept them alive.

"Existential despair did not germinate in the hell holes of Auschwitz or Siberia but rather in the cafés of Paris, the coffee shops of Copenhagen, the luxury palaces of Beverly Hills. After a trip into Eastern Europe during the Cold War, novelist Philip Roth reported *In the West everything goes and nothing matters. While in the East nothing goes and everything matters.*"

Philip Yancy says that a lot of conservative Christians treat Ecclesiastes with polite distaste as if it shouldn't be in the Bible but he sees it as a profound reminder of the limits of being human, it sets forth the inevitable consequences of a life without God at the centre.

But in this day and age is politics any better or worse if the leading politicians don't have God at the centre?

As Richard Coles says in *Restoring Faith in Politics*; "The fact is that many people perceive the Christian churches to be about as inviting as an MFI

Superstore. And just as many people would sooner eat off the floor than a pine country-style, self-assembly refectory table, so would they sooner seek spiritual guidance from Mystic Meg than the Archbishop of Canterbury. I think this matters; in the decade of evangelism, with Church attendance falling, with the under-forties about as unchurched as any demographic has ever been, we need to think about why people find the church so unattractive—or worse, why they don't feel anything at all about it." And exactly the same thing could be said of people's attitudes to politics.

What am I trying to say? That God matters in people's lives, yes; that in affluent societies God gets pushed to one side or forgotten or not needed, yes: that politicians make the decisions that affect the lives of many people, yes; that having a faith as a politician affects those decisions, maybe.

When I first set out writing *Onward Christian Socialist* the question asked of would-be publishers, was, who is the target audience? Was it aimed at a political readership or a Christian readership? Well both, I answered. Unfortunately, they said, that's not such a big market for selling books and making a profit; when you begin to mix politics with religion the target audience gets smaller and interest diminishes. Should my name have been Tony Blair or George Bush then such a book would have caused a considerable amount of interest if only to look into the psyche of a world leader. Unfortunately, my name is neither, or fortunately depending on your point of view.

For many people religion and politics not only shouldn't mix but actually don't mix. Desmond Tutu, however, spoke for many when he said, "I don't know which Bible people are reading when they say that religion and politics don't mix."

In the book *God's Politicians*, Graham Dale writes about senior political figures who have played a significant role within the British Labour Party from Keir Hardie through to the modern day.

He gives quotes, demonstrating that in times past it was no problem to profess your faith through politics. Keir Hardie would write in 1910 "The impetus which drove me first of all into the Labour movement and the inspiration which carried me on in it, has been derived more from the teachings of Jesus of Nazareth than all other sources combined."

And as R. H. Tawney explained his commitment to equality, "In order to believe in human equality, it is necessary to believe in God. It is only when one contemplates the infinitely great that human differences appear so infinitely small.... what is wrong with the modern world is that having ceased to believe in the greatness of God, it has to emphasise distinctions between men."

In the secular age that we now live in it would be deemed to be politically incorrect for leading politicians to utter such comments (except, of course, in the USA). Maybe at specific religious gatherings it would be acceptable but certainly not at political meetings. For those politicians who do try to express their faith, they get lampooned, ridiculed and mocked by the popular press, entertainers and the politically correct establishment. Although Ian Paisley wouldn't care what was said about him as the interview in Chapter 7 will show. But for many people, Ian Paisley is seen as a crank, troublemaker and epitomises all that is wrong with religion. So too is George Bush and his Attorney General, John Ashcroft, certainly viewed from this side of the Atlantic, they epitomise the religious right of the USA.

Tony Blair gets it from all angles, newspapers magazines, comedians, cartoons, yet he seldom mentions his faith publicly. Graham Dale again,

> *"Despite his faith being a compass for values and policy, Blair nonetheless remains reluctant to publicise it. He is quick to point out, as John Smith was before him, that Christianity has no monopoly on ethics, nor should all Christians necessarily be Socialists. According to those close to him, however, maintaining his faith and attending Communion are central disciplines and resources in his busy life. In 1991 for example, whilst on a visit to New York and after a late night of socialising, colleagues were surprised to see him up at the crack of dawn and setting off to find a church. Any reticence Blair displays in publicising his faith reflects his abhorrence of religion as a vehicle for electioneering and, as a politician, his sensitivity about the plurality of Britain's religious culture. Nevertheless, there is little doubt that it continued to inform his thinking and policies and contributed to his success as Shadow Home Secretary. Blair was now being widely talked of as the next leader of the Labour Party, but no one believed it would come so soon."*

It came so soon because of the untimely death of John Smith, the leader of the Labour Party who was the most open about his Christian faith. Once again thanks to Graham Dale. "He attended Cluny Parish Church in Edinburgh and his Christianity was prominent during his campaign for the leadership. He told

BBC Radio 4's *Sunday* programme, 'I am an active and professing member of the Church of Scotland... It gives meaning to my political activities, because you have a sense of obligation to others."

In March 1993 he delivered the annual Tawney lecture for *The Christian Socialist Movement* and concluded with these words:- "The second commandment calls upon us to love our neighbour as ourselves. It does not expect a frail humanity to be capable of loving our neighbours more than ourselves: that would be a task of saintly dimension. But I do not believe we can truly follow that great commandment unless we have a concept of care and concern for our fellow citizens which is reflected in the organisation of our society. In this vital way we can ally our Christian faith to our democratic socialist conviction. In the pursuit of both we can aspire to lead our country to find the real wealth which only a good society can provide."

John Smith was a good man and followed a long line of political leaders who were motivated by their faith.

So what am I trying to do with this book? Well, probably to show how faith does affect politicians and to show it from a perspective of people I have known or met over the 17 plus years that I was a Member of the European Parliament. It illustrates specific crises that people have gone through; it asks if prayer helps or does it matter; it looks at the why questions—why did God not answer my prayer? Why has this happened to me? Most of all it tries to show real-life people and what their relationship is with God or Jesus. Some are well known, others less so.

It also attempts to show that faith can't be inactive in politics, especially for those who have a personal relationship with God.

Several of those who were interviewed, especially those who have lived through oppressive regimes, make the same comment that it's the truth that sets you free. And it's through their faith that they seek the truth and eventually triumph.

Jim Wallis is the editor of *Sojourners* magazine and a social activist based in Washington. I remember reading somewhere that the British Chancellor of the Exchequer, Gordon Brown, had said his book, *The Soul of Politics*, had been an inspiration for him. I bought it and it was a great read. He quotes Gandhi warning against the seven social sins. He names them as politics without principle, wealth without work, commerce without morality, pleasure without conscience, education without character, science without humanity, and worship without sacrifice. He says these social sins today provide an apt description of our leading institutions and cultural patterns; they are the accepted practices of the life of modern nations.

Wallis goes on to say:

> *"What we seem to have lost is something as simple as respect—for each other, for the earth, and for the kind of values that could hold us together. Most of the social economic and political issues we now face have a spiritual core.*
>
> *"We need a politics that offers us something we haven't had in a long time; a vision of transformation. A new sense of direction will require a moral compass that we can trust. We must seek a 'politics of conversion', as Cornel West, an African-American Christian intellectual, has said. Jewish editor Michael Lerner hopes for a new 'politics of meaning'. Dare we seek the conversion of politics itself? What many today are trying to find is the **soul of politics**."*

And maybe that is what I'm trying to do with this book.

Another question asked by publishers is, is it for a European readership or a UK readership? Does it matter? I sigh. Well apparently it does. Now I have had several conversations with Europeans, from east and west, with South Africans, Americans and anybody else who I thought could give some insight into how they feel motivated to act in their political lives and I can't see how that should affect the readership. Having said that the Prologue probably needs a knowledge of how the European Parliament operates but if you don't have it, you can use your imagination.

At least the churches who get involved in European issues are certainly not disinterested in politics. In May 2001 at a Conference of European Churches held in Brussels, they published a paper entitled "Churches in the Process of European Integration." In it they said this:

> *"The process of European integration is a complex enterprise. Opening the borders between states and enabling free movement of people will result in intensive contacts between people and groups of different backgrounds, experiences and traditions. The development of a common Europe must not*

end, however, with the discussion of administrative technicalities. The European Commission recognised this at an earlier stage. The need to give the developing European Union a sense of direction and purpose as it moved beyond the single market to a political union—what Jacques Delors called 'giving a soul to Europe'—has been part of the ethos which surrounded European institutions for several years. At the present stage, however, much more needs to be taken into consideration. Churches are aware of it and on various occasions clearly expressed their position in this regard. The most recent document to cite is the statement which came from Rumania, signed by leaders of all Christian churches and of other religions in the country: 'Process of European integration can be completed only if economic dimensions will be accompanied by the spiritual dimension.' Ethical and spiritual dimensions of the future European construction are unavoidable requirements, if the process of European integration is to be successful."

If modern Europe and its Member States including the United Kingdom want to make the world a better place then they need a driving force, they need a soul. Who is "THEY," the politicians? The politicians have to reflect the wishes of the people, yes; the people who want more consumer power, cheaper goods, higher standards. But politicians also have to lead public opinion, not just to be led by it, and that comes across too, especially from the South Africa inputs into this.

Back to Jim Wallis and a speech he gave at a Faith in Politics Conference organised by the Christian Socialist Movement in 2001.

"Something is wrong in the United States. That is why faith-based organisations and faith communities have become involved. In the US we have a phenomenon of record prosperity and rising inequality at the same time. One in six of our children are poor in the richest country on the face of the earth. One in three children of colour are poor today in the US. Proverbs says that without a vision, what happens? Without a vision the people perish, and it is always the most vulnerable who perish first. The kids in my neighbourhood live twenty blocks from the White House and go to bed to the sound of gunfire at night. In Seattle there are now 10,000 millionaires, while the public schools are crumbling. I was in the cathedral to preach the night before the Seattle demonstrations in the street. We had a packed house, Jubilee 2000 people were there in force. And I shared with them something that is a hot topic I think for me these days and I am sure it is for you too. It's an insight from biblical archaeology.

"When they dig down in the ruins of ancient Israel, they find periods where the houses are more or less the same size. The artefacts of life show a relative equality between the people. During those periods the prophets are silent. No Amos, no Isaiah, no Jeremiah. When they dig down and find other periods where there are great houses and small shacks where the instruments of life show a great disparity between the people, that's when the prophets rise up and speak the justice and judgement of Yahweh.

"At the end of the illustration, I am often asked this simple question: 'Where are the prophets today?' That night in Seattle 2,000 people jumped out of their seats and said, 'We're here, we're here, we're here in Seattle.' Issues like Jubilee 2000 have become for us not just an economic issue, not just a moral issue, but really a religious issue and indeed a biblical issue. It reminds me of my favourite English theologian, Robin Hood."

So let's look for some prophets of today and what their message is. I've had the privilege of meeting many of them, hopefully within these pages you may get a glimpse of a few.

TWO

On 3rd May, 1979, two significant events occurred. Margaret Thatcher won her first general election and I was elected to Wigan Metropolitan Borough Council a.k.a. The Metro. After that date the Labour Party began a civil war and had some of its darkest days. The 1983 general election had Labour espousing an anti-European agenda, in the words of Eric Heffer, he of the National Executive Committee, "Make no bones about it, a vote for Labour is a vote to come out of Europe," or words to that effect. I always reckon that the 1983 general election was a second referendum on Europe. If a vote for Labour was a vote to come out, then there was an overwhelming vote against Labour, and by analogy, a vote to stay in.

After that election, I thought that I would never see a Labour government again. We had been blethered, well and truly stuffed. For the European elections of 1984, I had been nominated by the Leigh Constituency Labour Party to be a candidate for the Merseyside East European constituency, which comprised eight Westminster constituencies, including Leigh, where we lived at the time. At that time, the battles in the Labour Party with the Militant Tendency were raging and in order not to split the anti-Militant vote, I withdrew in favour of Ian McCartney, who had been nominated by the neighbouring Makerfield constituency.

Ian didn't win, Les Huckfield did. Les had been okay at one time. He'd been the youngest MP in the House of Commons and a Government Minister. He'd been in the mainstream of Labour politics and when the electoral Commission redrew the parliamentary boundaries, his safe seat of Nuneaton became unsafe. So he managed to get selected for the old Wigan Borough seat, where Alan Fitch MP, was retiring. Then the seats in Wigan were re-organised and he had to fight for the new Wigan seat. He lost. He was defeated in a run off with Roger Stott, a mate of mine, whose Westhoughton constituency seat was also about to disappear. Roger's agent was Ian McCartney and with the help of several Trade Unions, especially the EEPTU, led in Wigan by Ken

Jackson, they managed to get the votes for Roger.

I always maintain it was at this point that Les went, let's say, away from the mainstream.

Les spied his chance to go for the European Constituency seat of Merseyside East and with the help of the hard left and Militant, he was successful. I think it was then that I decided he wasn't going to be my MEP in 1989 when the next Euro elections came around.

Wigan wasn't the only Westminster seat he went for. He tried Knowsley North and Sedgefield, where a certain Tony Blair defeated him.

Five years later, the Labour Party had just about all its candidates in place for the 1989 European elections one year before the actual election date. Except that is for Merseyside East. In an attempt to save about three pages of this book, let's just say it took place virtually at the last minute with only weeks to go before the election. I'd been nominated by Leigh again and there were six candidates including Les.

A lot of prayer, a huge amount of prayer, went into this, strangely enough along the same lines of fifteen years later, i.e. if it be your will, help me not make a pillock of myself (maybe I didn't use the word pillock). There was an extra one; if I get it, let me make the job a crusade for doing good (sounds good and wanted to impress God).

The selection procedure, 10 minutes speech followed by 10 minutes of questions, was held in Haydock Number Two Labour Club. Six candidates, and I was drawn to go last, so the one hundred or more delegates had had nearly two hours of it before I got on. Let me give it to them, God. A speech so well rehearsed a professional actor could not have done it better. Questions and Answers, a piece of cake, forceful, not dodging any issues, being up front and honest, whether they liked what I said or not. As my twenty minutes finished I left the room, closed the door behind me and stood at the top of the stairs alone. I was so bursting with confidence, I punched my right arm in the air and said: 'Thanks, God, we've done it.'

And we had. I was the Labour candidate for Merseyside East, about to get a majority of 120,000 at the forthcoming European election. I was described in the Guardian as a "little known Councillor from Wigan" and I wasn't sure if they meant little as in stature and known all over Wigan, or (you know what I mean).

At the meeting of Labour candidates in London shortly afterwards, there was a photo shoot with the leader of the Labour Party, Neil Kinnock. We queued up and one by one went forward, shook hands, turned to the camera and smiled. My turn came, I offered my hand and as I said "Terry Wynn, Merseyside East," he grabbed me and hugged me and said, "A Labour gain already, even before the election." I think we can assume that Neil was highly delighted, it was after all one of the first victories in the fightback against Militant and not an insignificant event at the time.

Just as an aside, the first time I met Tony Blair, Roger Stott had invited him to Wigan in his role as Shadow Home Secretary. Roger introduced me and as we shook hands, he asked what had we three got in common. No idea I said. "We've all beaten Les Huckfield in a selection process," was his reply.

It's easy to get carried away and become big headed when you get selected for a seat that's rock solid Labour and is going to give you a living for the next five years. (I hadn't planned on more than one mandate in case Militant fought back.) But having the wife and family that I do, they made sure I kept, and have continued to keep, my feet firmly on the ground. Also, being an overt Christian meant it was pretty difficult to be aloof without accusations easily being thrown at you. My mug shot was everywhere in glorious techni-colour as the election posters went up. However, I was soon brought down to earth when I walked into one Labour Club as a pop group were performing on the stage. All around that club were my posters, but they had put one on the front of their base drum and added a Mikhail Gorbachov type birthmark to my forehead and I looked just like him. So as I entered the lead singer shouted into the microphone: "He's here, Gorbachov has just arrived." Laughter all over the place. Lesson to learn: keep a good sense of humour and don't take yourself too seriously.

On another occasion, I was being introduced to just about everybody to make sure I met as many people as possible. One Labour Club secretary introduced me to an elderly lady. Realising she was hard of hearing, he said in a very raised voice: "This is Terry Wynn," to which she replied, "When did you get of Beirut then?" Lost on the younger generation, but may be appreciated by Terry Waite.

At the time of writing, I've had the honour to be an elected representative in the European Parliament for 15 years. The 1994 election was fought with the same constituency, however, with a change to the name of Merseyside East and Wigan. Then in 1999 and 2004, the constituencies were scrapped and a Regional list system came into being with a Proportional Representation voting system. It came into being thanks to a Labour Government. The House of Lords sent it back to the Commons five times before it was agreed and very few people supported it but, according to hearsay, a deal had been done between the Prime Minister and the Liberal Leader, Paddy Ashdown, on the flight back from the Hong Kong handover ceremony. The Liberals gained a lot from it. What the Labour Party ever gained, I still fail to see. In 1999, I saw good men and women, who had been Labour MEPs, thrown to the wolves by their own party as our numbers went from 62 to 29. I said at the time, it was the worst case scenario; I was wrong. In 2004, with the number of UK seats reduced to 78 from 87 because of enlargement of the EU, the Labour delegation was reduced to 19.

Yet I am still one of those 19, and thankful to be so. Whenever I address an audience I try to get across the message that I have never forgotten who put me where I am or who pays my wages. And I always stress that I have the best job in the world. It has to be (rumblings of 'no wonder, with your salary and expenses'). To be given the chance to work in a multi-national environment, first with people from 12 different countries, then 15 and now 25, is something that not many people get the chance to do. You have to realise, appreciate and learn that there are at least 25 different cultures, 20 official languages, and things are not always done as they would be back home.

To vote on the things that matter, such as legislation or the budget, Parliament needs a qualified majority, no political group has the numbers to deliver on anything unless it gets the support of others. So when you are passing an amendment or trying to get a result, you have to persuade others of your arguments, you have to understand why they may vote the way they do, you have to learn how to compromise and make deals. Compared to British politics, it is much more complex and intriguing and the end result means the legislation not only affects your constituents, but people throughout Europe.

Another part of the excitement of the job and yet another privilege was that not long after I was first elected in 1989, the Berlin Wall came down. (I don't mean it came down because I was elected.) The Socialist Group met in the Reichstag next to the wall in January 1990 and we were the first Westerners to enter East Berlin through the Brandenburg Gate. We were led by the group

President Jean-Pierre Cot, and it's fair to say that Doris, my wife, was the very first woman to go through. From 1989, Europe has never stopped evolving and the European Parliament has played a major role in helping the integration of Europe, bringing its peoples together and the fifteen years since then have certainly been exciting times in Europe. Add to the fact that there are ample opportunities to travel and learn about different countries and their peoples, add to the fact that you can genuinely help people whom you represent with a variety of problems, then it has to be the best job in the world. Having said that, you also have to accept the weird letters and phone calls and the fact that when British newspapers write any articles about MEPs, the words "fraud," "gravy-train" and "expenses" will appear in it somewhere.

If politicians are seen as the lowest form of life, then let me assure you, when you have an 'E' between the 'M' and the 'P', then you're probably seen as being even lower. So lesson number two: you need a pretty thick skin to take the insults and when you get used to them (no, you never get used to them) or should I say, when you can accept that it's part of the baggage that goes with the role, then you can get on and do a good job.

As a Methodist local preacher, I often think when I look at the congregation that most of them look at me, after just having read the Mail on Sunday, and think he's some sort of crook and layabout, because that's the way MEPs are portrayed. So what's new? Join the queue as the press have a go at young people, sports stars, pop stars, royalty. It's part of British life, unfortunately.

The role of an elected representative is a privileged position, where you are expected to reflect the hopes and aspirations of the people who voted for you. As a local councillor, I represented an electorate of about 14,000 people; when I had a constituency it went up to 500,000 people, now that it's a Region stretching from Carlisle to Congleton, the figure is five million electors and a population of seven million in total. As you may have gathered, I don't like this PR, Regional List system; it makes me feel remote from the general public and also remote from Labour Party members, who do all the work to get me elected.

I actually like being with 'normal' people, grassroots people. That doesn't mean I baulk at the chance to meet the great and the good, Presidents, Prime Ministers, Alex Ferguson. I've dined with the Dalai Lama, which goes down well with the brown bread and sandals brigade; met Nelson Mandela and have a great photograph of the two of us, so that's always good for name dropping;

and been introduced to Bill and Hilary Clinton when he was President. Actually it was the most surreal experience. Doris and I had been invited to attend the National Prayer Breakfast in Washington. On the day of the Breakfast, which the President attended and spoke at, I was asked by Paul Petrie, who'd organised the invitations, to be in a specific room in the Hilton Hotel, where the event took place, at some time like 06.30, because the President normally met a dozen or so international guests. So I am stood there in this room chatting to some Albanian guy in French, next to Benazir Bhutto (she of Prime Minister of Pakistan fame) waiting to meet Bill and Hilary. All I could think about was what would they say in Platt Bridge if they could see me now (Platt Bridge being the place of my birth—see *Onward Christian Socialist* to get the feel of it being a working class, pit village). They appeared, we were introduced, chatted for a while, a camera clicked and they were off to Benazir. I never did get the photo, apparently his press people only made available those pics that flattered him. How many Platt Bridgers, North Westerners, Europeans, really get the chance to be in those situations? This really is a privileged position and has to be the best job in the world.

Unfortunately, a large section of the British press spend their time demonizing the EU, to such an extent that a sizeable portion of the population are turned off by any mention of the word Europe; speak to any women's institute or pensioners gathering and it soon becomes apparent. So part of the job is to defend the EU against the blitzkrieg of the *Sun, Mail, Star, Express, Telegraph*, Times and their regional offshoots. It's not easy, but I enjoy it. Being Daniel in the lions den has its thrills and it's good to put a positive case against all the negatives. The trouble is, for most people, when their minds are made up, facts only confuse the issue.

When people ask "What's Europe ever done for us?" it reminds me of that scene in the film 'The Life of Brian' where the group of zealots, led by John Cleese, are having a right good go at the Romans, when someone says "What have the Romans ever done for us?" "Well we have decent roads," someone replies. "Yeah, but apart from roads, what have the Romans ever done for us?" "We have a decent water supply thanks to aqueducts." "Yeah, but apart from roads and aqueducts, what have the Romans ever done for us?" "Well we have central heating." "Yeah, but apart from roads, aqueducts and central heating, what have the Romans ever done for us?" And so it goes on.

So what has Europe done for us? At this point I am supposed to rattle off all the job creating, economic regenerating projects and millions of pounds that have come into my region; I am supposed to stress that virtually all UK environmental legislation emanates from Europe, whether it be clean air, clean water, clean rivers, clean beaches, protected habitats or lead free petrol. I am supposed to show how the rights of consumers have benefited from EU membership, e.g. cheaper telephone calls, unified cell-phone systems, easy travel, have all benefited everyday people. Cheap air travel hasn't come about because Ryanair or Easy Jet thought that it would be a good idea. It came about because the EU broke the monopolies of the big airlines for the benefit of European travellers. We take for granted free movement of people, goods and services across Europe, as we do with rights at work and women's rights especially, all of which emanate from Europe. And it's also worth stressing that the EU is the single biggest donor of aid to the third world. All these things are good and worthy of stressing and are good for making a pro-European case to show what Europe has done for us. However, one thing, above all else, needs to be stressed and that is that the people of Europe have lived in peace for almost six decades. Mine is the first generation that has not been involved in a war in Europe. The history of this continent is littered with nations settling their differences with bombs, bullets, spears and bows and arrows. The fact that we have lived in peace for almost 60 years is nothing short of a miracle. There are those who say it is all down to NATO, but NATO kept the Russians out, it didn't go about reconciling people. The founding fathers of the EU were determined that countries with histories of fighting one another never went to war again. The foundations of the EU were built on creating peace and prosperity.

Whenever I speak to young people I usually ask them if they have seen two films; one is 'Schindler's List' and the other is 'Saving Private Ryan'. The former, which depicts the horrors of the Holocaust, shows events that were reality on this continent sixty years ago. Mankind seems to have an innate bestiality to do all kinds of atrocities to fellow human beings, and don't think that it is only in history. Events today in Bosnia-Herzegovina, Rwanda, Sudan show exactly the same kind of inhumanity. I've visited several of the Balkan trouble spots and in places like Kosovo, the hate between the two communities is tangible. Were it not for the EU police and military presence there, they would be tearing one another to pieces.

As for 'Saving Private Ryan', when I saw that film I couldn't breathe for the first half hour, which showed the brutal reality of war at the Normandy landings. It portrayed fear, horror, young men crying for their mothers, literally crapping themselves with fright and it showed the horror of war in all its gory detail.

Then I tell the young people to go to the graveyards of those Normandy dead, especially the American ones who lost so many, and those white crosses go on for ever. Then look at the ages of those buried there and its sixteen, seventeen, eighteen years old. Wars wipe out generations of young people.

The other place I recommend they go to is Ypres in Belgium to see the Menin Gate, that monument to British and Commonwealth dead in the First World War. The Menin Gate will bring a tear to any eye that sees it. It contains the names of 56,000, whose bodies were never found. How do you lose 56,000 bodies in four years? Because they get blown to smithereens, because they get trampled in the mud, because the rats eat them or the dogs eat them. That's the reality of war and that is what this continent has seen from time immemorial. With sixty years of peace has come prosperity. Countries such as Greece, Spain and Portugal not too long ago were military dictatorships, now they are thriving democracies with good economies thanks to the help of the EU. Of the ten new member states, three were actually part of the Soviet Union (Latvia, Lithuania and Estonia), five others had fifty years of totalitarian regimes. All now look to increasing their chances of prosperity and lasting peace thanks to the EU. They know that as part of the EU, as new democracies they can never go back to the totalitarian systems they knew. They want to be part of the EU so that they can guarantee their democratic rights, their human rights, their civil liberties and their freedom. As Rowan Williams, the Archbishop of Canterbury, said when he addressed a group of MEPs in the European Parliament, above all else the EU is a moral philosophy.

One of my Spanish colleagues once said to me: "I knew we had democracy when I could go to bed at night and not fear a knock on the door." No-one from the UK could ever imagine that type of situation and I touch on other similar people I've had the privilege of knowing in the following couple of chapters.

So when people ask "What has Europe done for us?" my answer wants to express this state of peace we now live in. Unfortunately, too many take it for granted and just want to dwell on the money that the UK either pays in or gets out of the EU. There is a great deal of Euro-scepticism in the UK, actually it's more than scepticism, it's cynicism, which I think is dangerous. As Oscar Wilde once said, a cynic is a person who knows the price of everything and the value of nothing.

I welcome the whole European project, that aims to bring people closer together rather than shouting insults at one another across closed borders. I have to say that this cynicism shows itself time and time again with constituents. There was a bloke from Wigan who wanted me to complain to the Spanish health authorities because the doctor he went to see whilst on holiday couldn't speak English and so couldn't treat him. "They should all be made to speak English" was his attitude. And when someone ends up in jail, usually for drug offences, the complaint is that the legal system of that country is deficient. That certainly applied to one Lancastrian, whose car had been impounded by the Belgian police after he and his son were stopped driving two cars full of contraband cigarettes. The real problem was that it was his disabled wife's Motability car.

Invariably the general public only make contact with my office when they have problems or when they want to complain and a lot do. Many are rude and arrogant, thankfully Marilyn, my PA, Secretary, problem solver, office manager and barrier between the complainants and me, knows how to deal with them in the politest of manners.

What is evident from fifteen years of doing this job is that there seems to be a tendency to moan and complain, blame someone else and to be impolite with it.

There are nice people of course and it's always pleasant when someone actually says thank you to Marilyn for some problem she may have solved, but those occasions are few and far between. We live in an era of people demanding their rights, but forgetting that with rights go responsibilities.

When I was a kid living in our terraced house in Platt Bridge near Wigan, every Autumn Silcock's travelling fairground would pitch camp for a few weeks on the spare land behind the house. The fun-fair would be set up and the caravans made their home in our village. We used to supply them with fresh water and got to know them quite well.

On top of one of the trailers, which were always highly decorated, were the words "Civility costs nothing but it means a lot." I never understood what it meant but as a kid it was fixed in my mind. Herbie Silcock, the owner, may have been illiterate, according to Dad, but that motto said a lot about him.

Just to go back to Jim Wallis again from Chapter 1, *"What we seem to have lost is something as simple as respect—for each other, for the earth, and for the kind of values that could hold us together."* A bit of civility towards each other would go a long way. And so it would if we applied it to our neighbours in Europe instead of seeing them as the 'divil incarnate'. There are those in the UK who would have our country be the "Neighbour From Hell" in this European neighbourhood, putting up high fences around our property, shouting at those who live nearby and criticising everything they do. The reality is that we do all have to live as good neighbours, helping each other, showing solidarity and trying to set common rules that we can all exist with.

Politicians are probably second only to clergymen (and women) for people bringing their problems to them. The difference being that the Clergy have a far bigger load with far more complex, human, spiritual problems.

During elections, when knocking on doors, that's when people can really have a go. Being honest, the vast majority of people are very pleasant on the doorstep. However, my favourite canvassing story concerns Lyndsay Hoyle the MP for Chorley. Lyndsay was knocking on doors during the 2001 General Election campaign when an old lady answers the door:-

"Good morning love, I'm Lyndsay Hoyle, the Labour Party candidate, just calling to see if you'll be voting Labour," he says.

"Labour? Labour? What's Labour done for pensioners?" she asks.

"Well we reduced VAT on domestic fuel from 15% to 8%."

"Big deal" or words to that effect.

"Well, we've given a free TV licence to the over 75s."

"I'm not over 75," she retorts.

So Lindsay comes in with the *coup-de-grace* "What about the £200 winter fuel allowance that everyone over 60 gets."

"Winter fuel allowance! Winter fuel allowance," she retorts. "It's been so cold, I've had to spend it on mi heating."

There is no pleasing some folk.

At this point, I should relate my two favourite stories about elections. The first one was during a local election in Platt Bridge in the seventies. There was, and still is, an elderly persons' home known as Sherwood House. I had been down there and thought that I had ensured everyone had a postal vote. On election day, someone came into the Labour Party Committee Room to ask if I could take my car to return two elderly ladies from the polling station back to Sherwood House. These two had walked half a mile up-hill, using zimmer frames, to vote Labour in a rock solid Labour seat. I began to mildly scold them for doing such a thing, when one of them said "Listen young man," which I took as a compliment for someone having turned 30, "I can remember the time when women didn't have a vote and I've never failed to vote since."

The second concerned the 2001 general election and I was helping in Leyland in the South Ribble constituency. I was asked to take my car, pick up an elderly lady at a certain address, take her to the polling station then take her home. When I arrived at the door and rang the bell, she answered, clutching her side and was in obvious pain. I asked what was wrong and she said she had slipped and fallen and had probably cracked a rib. I immediately offered to take her to the hospital but she refused, "If I go there first I may not get out for some time. Take me to vote so I don't miss it, bring me back here and I'll call for the doctor," which I did.

Nothing galls me more than people who say "I never vote" and young people are the ones who are the worst offenders. Yet many young people do care, even if it is about single issue items, like animal welfare or the environment. What politicians are failing to do is to connect with them to give them a vision of that soul that nations and the EU need and to show them that they should be standing up and declaring themselves as the prophets.

On the other hand after a week of canvassing, I go to our church in Standish and meet Bill Jones, an octogenarian who radiates friendliness, warmth and his Christian faith. Bill is always smiling, always cheerful, always thankful for what God has given, even if it's a simple sunny morning. Bill Jones and people like him do my heart good,. If only I could spread whatever Bill has around, not only to the UK but across Europe, then Europe really would have a soul. And it can be spread around, what it needs are those who are prepared to do it. So where are the prophets? Let's have a look in the following pages.

THREE

At the height of the BSE crisis in the UK, the beef industry was taking quite a battering. Most of the world wasn't buying British beef and the EU had placed a ban on beef exports from the UK to other member states. Irish beef was not affected and so in a debate on the issue of BSE in the European Parliament at a Strasbourg plenary session, the Reverend Ian Paisley, MEP for Ulster took the floor to speak. For the sake of accuracy I should research into the records to find out what his exact words were, but that may spoil the story. My lasting memory is of Ian standing and saying in that wonderful Northern Irish accent: "Mr President, the people of Ulster are British, but the cows are Irish and should therefore be exempt from the ban." It's moments like that which are to be treasured.

Or the time Otto Von Hapsburg, the last Crown Prince, the eldest son of the last Emperor of the Austro-Hungarian Empire (who is a wonderful person and at the time of writing is 90 years young and still going strong, though not now an MEP), walked into the Members' bar to see everyone watching the TV.

"What is going on?" he asked.
"It's a football match," his colleague replied.
"And who is playing?" enquired Otto.
"Austria and Hungary."
"And who are they playing against?"

Absolute gems.

Like any establishment that has lots of people working in it, there are people like Ian and Otto who add character to the place. The European Parliament had and still has its fair share of former Presidents, Prime Ministers, pop stars, sports stars and names to remember like Danny ("the Red") Cohn-Bendit. One New Zealand Green MP, who was visiting the parliament once, enthused to me how she had met one of her heroes from the sixties and I realised it was

Danny from his Paris student-riot days.

The majority are not household names, just hard working people in the main, who I get the chance to work with. Like for instance, Bárbara Dührkop Dührkop, of Swedish, German descent, who is an MEP for Spain. Bárbara became an MEP when her politician husband was assassinated on the doorstep of their home by ETA terrorists in the Basque country. She, in effect, took on his mantle. Even now she has police protection when in Spain, ever since she was found to be on the ETA hit-list. I've known her for fifteen years and we are good friends. Recently, whilst visiting the North West region of England, as we drove along the M6 Motorway, she saw the usual roadside sign 'No Hard Shoulder for 50 yards'. "What does that mean?" she asked. I pointed out what the hard shoulder was and that it disappeared for 50 yards. "What did you think it meant?" I asked. "I thought it was an instruction to relax. Like relax your shoulders, take out the tension," which shows how language can have different meanings for different cultures.

Bárbara and I have spoken about God and belief on several occasions. I once mentioned Bárbara's situation to a mutual acquaintance to say how she is an atheist because she has trouble believing in a God of love. His reaction was: "It's not that she doesn't believe in God, she just doesn't like Him."

He said it at the monthly Prayer Breakfast that is held in Strasbourg where Christian MEPs, assistants and any visitors can meet together and discuss a piece of scripture and its relevance to the situation we find ourselves in.

The Prayer Breakfast was started shortly after the first group of MEPs were directly elected in 1979. The format is that one of the MEPs will pick a short reading of Scripture and everyone is free to comment on it, then this is followed by a short period of intercessionary prayers. It lasts maybe fifty minutes but I have to say it is one of the most satisfying bits of my monthly calendar. It is so good to sit, eat, talk and share together with Christians from other denominations, traditions and countries.

People not only open up in sharing their faith, but share their doubts also, as was the case when I raised Bárbara's situation.

In the political families i.e. the political groups within the Parliament, the centre right PPE group (People's Party of Europe—at one time the old

Christian Democrat group but these days made up of all kinds of delegations) are by far the best at nurturing young talent from central and eastern Europe. For many years they have, using a Foundation created for that very purpose, brought young political leaders from across the old Iron Curtain countries to Brussels and Strasbourg as Stagiaires i.e. trainees, for a month or so work experience. Many of these young people, usually graduates, would attend the Prayer Breakfast in Strasbourg and make good contributions. The person charged with their responsibility, Stephen Billar, a British Tory, a very pro-European Tory I must add, once made the point that the families of these young people had been able to teach them their faith during the 50 years of Communist totalitarianism. What an achievement that was, to have been brought up in countries where religion was not only frowned upon but persecuted and to have come though a system where those of faith risked so much to pass on to their children their beliefs. For many of us we can't even begin to imagine what that must have been like.

In my previous book, *Onward Christian Socialist*, I mentioned Ulrich Meisel. I first interviewed him in the early nineties, when he was in the Parliament as one of the eighteen East German Observers prior to the 1994 elections. A decade later I spoke to him again.

His Christian upbringing in East Germany meant that he never succumbed to Communist Party indoctrination. He became a Methodist local preacher, and refused to do military service. He explained that "Eastern Germany was the only country in the Soviet Bloc which had a law that gave the freedom of choice for conscientious objectors not to go to the Army." Instead they were forced to do hard labour, dangerous activities for which workers were hard to find. "The overwhelming majority of conscientious objectors were either devoted Christians or they were connected with Christian groups. It was relatively simple for a Christian to be a legitimate conscientious objector, saying, 'I am a Christian and the Christian faith is against weapons and war'. You can read it in the gospel and they accepted it." However, it was less justifiable for an atheist to refuse to join a Communist army.

He explained how life in the former GDR was monotonous, there were no possibilities to change anything, to move to another town or get a different job. The churches provided the only forums for discussions on how to improve the quality of life. "In the early 80s in East and West Germany and most of Europe too, the churches started prayers for peace." However, when weapons were installed on both sides, the emphasis of the meetings changed from solely peace-related questions, to more general political questions, including the internal problems of the former GDR. Ulrich was a Methodist member of a working group in the *Ecumenical Assembly for Justice, Peace and the Integrity of Creation*, which set out to discuss such problems. He said it was in these meetings that the first voices spoke out against the power of the government.

In the Stalin era the church encountered much repression, but after his death, deStalinisation entailed a relaxation in certain policies. Practically this meant that, "inside the churches they were free to discuss all the political themes...the churches were the place where people could speak frankly about a lot of things which were taboo. It wasn't possible to discuss the environment in public, but it was in the churches. It was always connected with the questions of faith too, because you need a lot of hope to go forward under a dictatorship." The churches' activities were seen to be distinct from political activities from the state's point of view, so very few people were actually sent to prison because they became politically active within church groups.

This movement of which he was a part started officially in February 1988 and involved about half a million people. The final papers of the working group were discussed in May 1989, and the churches were packed. They were not expecting to be able to dramatically reduce the government's power, but "to take part of the power for civil right movements," and to ameliorate communism. During the discussions Ulrich told me, "Many people who were either not church members or church members only on paper came to worship at Christmas and to join church meetings and were very interested." When the churches spoke of justice, peace and the integrity of creation in God's name, it struck a chord with people outside the church, living in an officially atheistic state. "The last years before the wall came down the numbers of people coming to worship and even the numbers of church membership increased, after a long period of decreasing under Communist pressure." Here the roots were put down for 1989's non-violent revolution. In Ulrich's words, "We have seen in our lifetime, literally, the walls of Jericho falling down with people playing guitars. The Berlin wall, you see, was built on sand, not on justice, peace and the integrity of creation."

Before the wall came down he said the nature of the demonstrations began to change. The original motto for the movement and its related institutions was 'We are the people', this then changed to 'We are one people', referring to the desire for reunification. Ulrich believes that the change in emphasis happened too fast, and people fell away from political life. Yet the church still had a large role to play. During the revolution the Methodist church was very politically active. Ulrich explained that this was because "the only persons trained in democratic behaviour were members of church conferences and church lay leaderships. Our church conferences have democratic systems. The first President of the first free elected German Parliament was previously the Church Parliament President of a regional Lutheran Synod. The Think Tank of the Churches was more or less the leadership of the first free elected parties." After the wall came down, many Christians went into party politics; "Even in regions where only 5%–10% of the population was a member of any Christian church on paper, more than 50% of the first generation of party activists of all new democratic parties came from Christian backgrounds."

I asked Ulrich how his faith made a difference to his life under communism. "On one point there was hope to work, in the time of Iron Curtain where really nobody expected that things will change. The possibility existed that over my lifetime I would never make a good career because I am a Christian and I would never influence many people because we were cut off from any media. To reach even a certain level wasn't possible without being a party member, so you need a strong hope to say like St. Peter when he was called to fish in the centre of the lake in Nazareth, 'We have worked all over the night and there was nothing, but because I believe in you I will go again to this place.' The other point was a kind of freedom because to say from the beginning I am a Christian and my first boss is not the party leader or the dictator gave a certain kind of frankness that was very helpful."

After German reunification, he was one of the eighteen East Germans designated as official observers in the European Parliament. Because of his church work, he currently does not have time for party politics, but he is still active in the political scene. He is involved with many organisations that seek to influence political decision–makers, what he terms, "pre-political work." The main organisation he is a member of is the Church and Society Commission of the Conference of European Churches. 24 members represent nearly 200 European churches. Ulrich pointed out that if a representative from the organisation travels to any country there is always a Foreign Minister there to meet them.

According to Ulrich, "Germany is not really a Christian country," even though Johann Rou, "a very devoted Christian," was elected President. Ulrich believes that in the previous generation being a Christian in Western Germany was "a strong plus," but now is "a small minus". "We struggle against a society which is very materialistic indeed. It is sometimes harder than to struggle with the communist dictatorship. Before German reunification, the evil was institutional, now the evil is the regime of money." In the midst of such a society, Ulrich believes, "The face who could combat and overcome the 'existing socialism' will also overcome the materialism of the so called market economy." He explained Marxist ideology was held as almighty 12 years ago, now the market is seen as almighty, but "I think God is almighty and that is the main point and we have learned that from history and will learn that again."

This is a person with deep insight. His final comments make one think about the kind of society that we do live in, where he considers that for a Christian the battle against a materialistic world is harder than the battle against a dictatorship.

As stated before for many of us brought up in the West, who take so much for granted, we can't begin to imagine what others may have gone through.

★ ★ ★ ★

Each year in the Parliament there is a European Prayer Breakfast, where two to three hundred parliamentarians from across Europe, ambassadors, NATO staff, civil servants from the EU institutions and others, meet together in Brussels. It's not an easy event to organise and every time someone in Parliament's administration always tries to put a spanner in the works either because of security reasons or sound system problems but each year it goes off successfully. It is a wonderful occasion and it is good to meet with Christians from across Europe in this way. It always has good music, good fellowship, good food and good contributions from those who read and speak. I'm sure it scares the pants off the secularists.

There is a guest speaker to address those gathered there and I have had the opportunity of interviewing several of them. Tunne Kelam and Maat Laar are from Estonia, a country that was part of the Soviet Union, Boris Trajkovski, the President of Macedonia and Tony Hall, now the US Ambassador to the World Food Programme in Rome. In addition, there was an interview with Vytautas Landsbergis from Lithuania. All these made fascinating listening. For the four Europeans, I now want to give some idea of what they went through and what their faith meant to them during the times of oppression. Tony Hall I'll touch on in a later chapter.

★ ★ ★ ★

Tunne Kelam's father had been involved in politics and was a Lutheran minister, but his church was shut down at the end of the 1950s. He was also Secretary of the Estonian Christian Endeavour Movement. "He was a central figure of this movement during 1920s and 30s, and I remember he told me he had visited Lloyd George after the end of the First World War." His father would listen to foreign radio broadcasts, "a source of independent information" and Tunne followed his example, beginning to be interested in politics whilst at university. "I inherited the same interest. I started to listen to the English BBC language broadcasts and these formed my understanding of politics because I could receive independent information...this enabled me to build up an independent mind...I became familiar with western or democratic vocabulary. We were an occupied country under a terrorist totalitarian regime and it was in everybody's interest to think how we could regain our freedom." Thousands were arrested because they were felt to present a threat to the totalitarian power, even without proof of their opposition to the system. Freedoms were suppressed, religions persecuted, and "tens of thousands deported to Siberia within one week." Tunne estimated that one half of the Parliamentarians who were elected in the 1920s and 1930s were executed under the Communist regime. I once read an article that he wrote on the 60th Anniversary of VE Day in which he said:

"I saw Estonia invaded by the Red Army. As an eyewitness to the subsequent general marauding and destruction, I still remember the words of the Soviet captain who entered the farm where my family was staying in September 1944: 'My soldiers are not the worst ones you should be afraid of. But beware of the NKVD (later KGB) troops who follow us—they are the ones you should be afraid of.' In an effort to make human contact and to forestall the Soviet officer's obvious desire to grab my father's watch, my parents had started a conversation with him in Russian and also put my two-year-old brother on his lap. Frustrated in their attempts at this farm, the captain and his unit then raided the neighbouring one and took by force everything they wanted—as victors they felt it all belonged to them.

"Sadly, the Soviet captain's warning very soon came true. In the first five years after its 'liberation,' Soviet-occupied Estonia, with a population of one million, saw the arrests of 65,000 individuals on political grounds. Of those, many thousands were murdered outright or died in concentration camps. In just one month, March 1949, 22,000 persons were deported from their homes to Siberia while about 10,331 who were also on the lists, managed to hide themselves, but lost all their property. Most remained outlawed for years.

"The real experience for those of us living in Soviet-'liberated' Eastern Europe was deprivation of all civic freedoms and any right to a democratic and independent state. Estonia was subjected to intensive Sovietization and Russification which brought the Estonian people to the brink of becoming a minority in our own country.

"Tragically for Central and Eastern Europe, the coming of the Red Army did not mean restoration of freedom. On the contrary, it simply meant the replacing of one form of murderous dictatorship with another. It also meant being totally cut off from the rest of Europe by the Iron Curtain, unable even to cry for help. What really happened in those countries under the long years of Soviet domination is only now reaching a wider audience in a reunited Europe.

"Hundreds of thousands of Soviet POWs, who managed to survive German captivity, were not freed but were immediately sent to Gulag prison camps. They were 'guilty' because they had survived. So they were treated as traitors or potential German spies. Such contempt by the victorious Soviet regime for its own people tells all. The number of Gulag inmates more than doubled during the period immediately following the war.

"In Central and Eastern Europe, the first five years after the defeat of the Nazis saw at least one million persons killed during the formation of 'peoples' democracies.' The left-over Nazi concentration camps did not suffice—additional camps had to be built to accommodate the hundreds of thousands of new political prisoners."

So under this system he had to live.

He was never a member of a political party but became a lecturer in International Affairs under Kruschev, when the system was sufficiently liberal for him to speak critically of the Communist government. "I became very popular so I had authority and they trusted me...so I could work and try to bring independent objective information quite different from the Soviet propaganda to thousands of people." Eventually, after 8 years of teaching, his lectures were banned at the end of the 60s. "I got information because of the Polish papers I received, I learned Polish, then I learned Italian because *Communist Unita* was the best Communist paper we received. I tried to bring to the people as much information about Czech Revolution, the reform of the Communist Party as possible, and finally I was suppressed."

Tunne began to gather together a group of intellectuals and in 1972 they wrote a memorandum "based on international law and UN covenant and asked for their help to evacuate the Soviet occupation troops to implement their articles of the Atlantic Charter also for the Baltic States and to organise free elections." They then smuggled the document abroad. "It was the first systematic political document for many years arriving from occupied Estonia." The group also wanted to prove "that not 99.9% of Estonian population were supporting the Communist Party. Five of my friends were arrested, they were condemned to six years imprisonment for slandering of the Soviet Union." Half a year later Tunne was interrogated by the KGB and they confiscated his Estonian language Bible. "It had been printed in the UK and imported— Bibles were illegal of course." He discovered that he had been sacked from his job as the Senior Editor of Estonia Encyclopaedia and he then worked for ten years as a night watchman in a state owned chicken farm near Tallinn. He explained that the job brought "the advantage of having plenty of free time, which was most valuable and pleasant, to organise your time freely," despite being under continuous surveillance. He once jokingly said that as a vegetarian he was probably sent there so he wouldn't eat the chickens.

His political work carried on throughout the 1970s and 1980s in spite of the change of scene, "mediating information about human rights violations...in the Soviet Union through the West and receiving information from the West and occupied Estonia. I organised groups of intellectuals who gathered and discussed the situation and options and finally we reached the year 1987 when we organised the first open political demonstration in Tallinn. It was to commemorate the anniversary of Molotov/Ribbentrop Pact of 1939 which sealed the fate of the Baltic States and Finland and parts of Poland. The point was to press for the disclosure of the secret articles of this pact...it was interesting we didn't ask for freedom or for democracy because it was too risky at that time. We did ask for truth and in Estonia it happened that truth makes you free. We asked for the truth which what happened to us in 1940. Was it legal marriage to the Soviet Union as it was claimed or was it an occupation as a result of a deal by two dictators?

"Interestingly within one year even Mr. Gorbachov, who first denied having any documents about this pact managed to discover in the archives at Kremlin two copies of Russian version of this pact...it became clear that we are not rightfully or legally part of the Soviet Union. We had very significant moral support from the Western democracies who never recognised officially the annexations of the Baltic States. Actually it was our lifeline because the knowledge that it's not considered legal and it had a very concrete influence upon the behaviour of Moscow because the special treatment of the Baltic States made Moscow's rulers always more hesitant, after Stalin of course...being cautious of the possible Western reaction. In August 1988 we formed the first political party in the whole of the Soviet Union, which was called Estonian National Independence Party. The reformed communists pretended that they don't intend to separate from the Soviet Union, they only want more autonomy, cultural and economic and they support perestroika."

"In Estonia we declared honestly that 'We want restoration of independence and democracy.' It was considered crazy. I think we managed to do it because We were able to start and lead mass democratic initiatives, electing in 1990 a Congress of Estonia, a temporary democratic Parliament, of which I was President for two years, which had the right to decide about the basic questions...finally in August 1991, we managed to reach a national understanding between the Supreme Soviet and the Congress of Estonia to restore independence, not to proclaim independence of Soviet Estonia under the leadership of the Communist Party but to restore independence on the basis of legal continuity as it was restored after Nazi occupation in Denmark and the Netherlands."

Tunne told me "many people were surprised" that under Communism the Christians were "able to retain our balance and our quiet optimism and...didn't become angry and desperate... that was because of our faith. Our churches played a significant role. Churches were infiltrated of course by the Soviet Authorities and they tried to make some ministers their agents... they spied the churches continuously. During every Sunday Service there was a regular spy sitting in the church and writing down what the minister was speaking." Tunne said he knew "dozens of brave ministers and preachers who engaged not only in preaching and religious activities but who were involved also in political activities." The Estonian churches also had outside help, a Mission run by Richard Wurmbrand which provided Bibles and religious literature to help people living under Communism, and "Finnish activists brought in secretly thousands and thousand of Bibles."

Tunne explained that these 'religious tourists' also brought political literature with them, and "took our messages to the West, which were also political ones, it's part of the game, you can't separate the struggle for independence and human rights from religion." He saw that the church played "a vital role in regaining freedom and democracy," and also that "the belief that God is able to do anything, even the impossible, was the source of our moral strength, that we didn't become desperate and that our nation was able to avoid any hatred, any vengeance, to avoid any national clashes. The potential was there, there were tens of thousands of Soviet troops…of Russians who were very hostile to any idea of Estonian independence… they treated it as high treason." Tunne talked of being able to survive as a Christian under communism, "because we were able to retain a moral balance" by not being extremist. He believes that "one key to win the Russian understanding and support" was by honestly declaring their goals. Russian citizens also appreciated the Estonians' lack of hostility towards them.

He went on to tell me, "I try to mention God in my political speeches often, it's not a secret. I profess my faith openly." Unusually, in Estonia the press is so indifferent towards religion that "they don't notice politicians presenting their beliefs," despite it still being unusual for someone to do so. Tunne told me that he prayed often, saying, "I am very grateful that my faith has become an active one…because of politics and especially after losing my chances to become the President of the Republic." After losing that election Tunne and his wife began to pray every day. "My wife was not very religious before that but now we can't pass a day when we don't pray together twice. In a morning we never leave our house before praying together and we never went to sleep before praying and we have developed a habit of praying for all the people we have met during the day…We have been very grateful for this political loss because of so much bettering of our spiritual life." They came to see that what is important is "honesty, integrity and ability to understand," and that life is not about satisfying your own desires, "not a question of our individual career," but that you "have to trust God even when you don't succeed."

There is a lovely anecdote to his story. One of the radio stations he had listened to during the Soviet times was the Voice of Free Estonia and the first time that he went to the USA he met the "voice" that had relayed the news of the free world to him and his countrymen. They fell in love and she became his wife.

I was disappointed that I didn't become President of the European Parliament, yet here is a man who could have been President of his country and those final words resound in my ears, as I re-read them. He really does put things in perspective.

★ ★ ★ ★

One of Tunne's prodigies was Maat Laar and since Estonia achieved independence, government has for most of the time been in his hands. He is widely regarded as being responsible for Estonia's recent success. Young people went to church in Estonia during Communism merely to protest against the system. Maat Laar explained, "We often turned to the church, even not having smallest idea how they can support it because it was something which was forbidden." The churches were only full "at Christmas time, otherwise they were quite empty...quite often the Soviet system made everything to keep them empty, so the churches were economically suppressed... they don't have, for example, the youth work, it was not allowed, or any publications, everything was forbidden." Many people attended church simply "to show their anti-Soviet feelings," but it carried a high risk, you could easily be expelled from school for example. One of Maat's friends studied law, and then was expelled after he got married in a church. However, this did not discourage him and he eventually became a priest.

Maat began to go to church when he was a student. He said that it was the time of life when you examine your "way of life and what is important." However, it changed from merely being an expression of protest. "If you were there and started to hear...it started to develop. So...one moment I found that I was not only going to the church only in the Christmas time but I am visiting it in the ordinary days as well." Maat's faith came "step by step." "Suddenly found that I am a Christian and I must...take those necessary steps to really to be a Christian." It was a significant decision to become a Christian; "because...church was very hunted in the Soviet Union."

Politics was part of life in Estonia under the Communist occupation, though Maat was never a member of the party. "There was, in my young age, some totally stupid idea to join the communist party to try to destroy it from the inside, but...if you will unite yourself with the devil then actually you will never win...and so the people who tried even to do this they...didn't succeed very much." Rather than be involved in party politics he preferred to write history books, "about restoring Estonian history and giving the memory back in different eras." He wrote for the underground press as a student. He published his first book about Estonian history and it was smuggled out of Estonia and read in Free Europe and then published in different Western countries. Maat told me, "I was the first who raised the question about the Soviet crimes, and...then I got even to the *Pravda* to be officially accused of telling the dirty lies about the Red Army, and the KGB activities." They tried to jail him but the movement for independence had too much support and they didn't want to risk sparking off an uprising.

There were many cultural movements in Estonia which built the basis for the "mental resistance" against the Soviet system. Maat was an organiser within a movement fighting against cultural oppression, which was eventually disbanded by the KGB. He believes that memory "was the main battlefield, because like in George Orwell's 1984, 'who controls the past, controls the future'. And so the fight for the past was the very heart in those times. So our task was to keep their memory...alive. And we succeeded in this." He was expelled from the university "for just being...not enough soviet...for student activities." His next job was as a schoolteacher, and after two weeks he received his first visit from the KGB. Maat described the KGB as an "interesting organisation...They were sometimes not very *intellectually developed*." He talked about Gorbachev's perestroika reforms, "forgetting that the democracy is like a toothpaste; if you let it out, you couldn't put it back any more...and as he made this mistake then we used this, of course, and we launched step by step, bit by bit...the...organisations which will then start from the cultural, and finish in the politics."

When I asked him how he became Prime Minister without party politics he replied, "I don't know actually, I never wanted to be the Prime Minister, to be very frank, it just happened one time." As the first elections approached Maat was involved in building a union of small political parties. At the start "everybody had a very small support and as we started our campaign then we had very, very small support, no real big success, for...possibilities for success but in two months we turned to be the winner, which was big surprise I must say, biggest surprise for myself." He only realised the morning following the vote that he would become the Prime Minister.

Maat believes that the rules of politics in Estonia are "how they were some hundred years ago"; little has changed over the 13 years he has been a politician. "You must be very careful. And at the same time I think the politics needs very much the people with the Christian faith because...otherwise it become too dirty." Maat also explained that a Christian can ask God for forgiveness, which "makes…life easier." He told me that if God has put you in a position of power, then you should do the job to the best of your abilities. He compared the power at his disposal as a politician as possessing one of the rings in Tolkein's book *Lord of the Rings*. Maat believes his faith is essential for him in politics. "You have this ring of power somewhere, and you know if you use it you will be enormously powerful, you can crush this or crush that, and do this do that, but you will…step by step cease to be the human being…to have it here but not to use this…demands quite strong Christian faith, I must say."

I asked him how public he made his faith. He replied, "I never use this as some part of the campaigning but…it's quite public that I am Christian." In Estonia, being a Christian is negative for a politician because people perceive Christians as being weak, and they want their politicians to be "strong and powerful." However, "at the same time…it's very good for yourself, and if you're a Christian, you shouldn't really…hide it in any way." As politicians we've got some pretty awful decisions to make—you can rarely sit on the fence. Maat agreed and said that making tough decisions are when you need faith most. First of all he listens to his heart, then he prays about the decision. He told me it is also helpful to "have friends who are praying for you. If you can pray with somebody together…it's enormously important." He believes he would not have been as politically active under communism if it were not for his faith. His faith kept him strong and gave him confidence; "You know always that you are right and they are wrong."

★　★　★　★

Vytautes Landsbergis has a different story. His was not a fight for freedom from within the church or with a burning faith, but someone who felt the presence of a higher power as he ascended the steps to address a mass rally in Vilnius.

Professor Landsbergis became involved in politics gradually through his profession as a 'musicologist' in Lithuania; he was not a member of the Communist party. He explained that "together with colleagues of my own generation we wanted to change something and to act more freely, in more democratic ways." The changes they made were "step-by-step"; first of all they fought for a greater freedom of the press. "Changes were small, but they could grow and bring the desire for greater and essential changes… liberty and independence," which had always been their ultimate aim. Landsbergis' generation remembered independent Lithuania and the 10 years of armed resistance after the Soviet occupation, which was finally crushed in 1954. From then on, cultural activities were to all intents and purposes a clandestine activity. One sculptor was expelled from the union of artists because he made a sculpture of St. Christopher for one of Vilnius' churches. Religious freedom was very limited. "It was very much reflected in the underground publication, 'Chronicle of the Lithuanian Catholic Church', which was published for more than 10 years and sent to the West, distributed and translated in various languages...the KGB could not destroy it. Almighty KGB could not enter inside and destroy it." Going to church however "was not a risk for elders. It was a professional risk for teachers to participate in church services and to go." Priests were forbidden to teach catechisms; "They were sentenced harshly for it. So children could not be educated in religion." Landsbergis respected religion and Jesus Christ's teaching, but he did not go to church at that time, as he explains, "I was not a heart believer then." His opinions changed, "Together with a movement of liberation, when I felt that we were entering into a very risky period with great responsibility, because it could be turned into bloodshed. All could live calmly in slavery without any misfortunes." But as a leader he held the responsibility for what may happen to the people he was leading.

"Independence was not openly discussed at the meetings of intelligentsia...we had quite a great number of people previously deported or sentenced, spending long years in gulags and still deprived of rights." The movement for change was made up of "semi-clandestine groups of people of common mind. Those who could trust each other. Such groups could be of 6 or 10 persons. But we were cells of freedom...[we had] a moral approach to each other and to communication." Among the other groups in opposition to the Communist regime were environmentalists and those fighting for the preservation of culture heritage. Sajudis (The Lithuanian Reform Movement) was established on June 3rd, 1988, after the disparate groups realised that it was necessary to unite, and saw the example of the Estonian Popular Front, created in the spring of 1988. Sajudis was not really a party, rather "an umbrella organisation for all striving for the general goal." The organisation already had contact with the Communist party leadership and they worked towards increased co-operation with those in the Communist leadership who were also reform-minded. Landsbergis was not chairman at this time, but he was chosen by his colleagues to make an address to a mass rally in Vilnius on the 24th June, 1988. "We knew that just beyond us is the Ministry of Interior full of armed people prepared to crush this rally at the Cathedral square, as happened half a year later in Tblisi...the moment... I remember very well this moment when I wanted some support form a higher authority before going to the podium ...I made the sign of the cross...for myself. It was impulsive but something moved me to it from inside." Now Landsbergis described himself, at this time, as "agnostic," in the way that Pope John Paul II defined it.

"It was the beginning of the movement for liberation, but we continued the fight for very concrete goals, not claiming full independence. It was maybe wise I think not to put your head in the guillotine...We always claimed that we are for reforms, as Gorbachov in Moscow—we wanted openness, we wanted truth, we wanted democratisation and reform—perestroika. Something had to be restructured, but a little bit later, when we had been asked about what was the ultimate goal of perestroika in our mind, it is freedom to make a choice; people on the ground—let them think, discuss and say." Independence was always on the agenda but not usually expressed explicitly. "When the founding congress of our movement was held in Vilnius, 22nd October, 1988, in the programme this word 'independence' was not used—but liberties to express, to decide ourselves." Landsbergis' father, a veteran of the wars for independence, was invited to open the congress as the most aged person there at 95 years old. "He addressed the great congress, about 4–6,000 representatives from all Lithuania, including Communist party leadership, invited as guests. We were very open. And he said 'For what sake are we here? We are here to restore independence to Lithuania.' And what was even maybe more remarkable, it was the opening of monument of liberty in Kaunas, destroyed by Communists, but restored in this wave of perestroika and liberation." On the first hours of the 16th February 1989, the Goal of Sajudis—independence of Lithuania was proclaimed. This date was also the same date that Lithuania had declared independence in 1918. In the early morning of the 16th a declaration was adopted, in which independence was described as 'a right to live in an independent way, rejecting any dictate on the nation.' Then we went to the cathedral in Kaunas, where Holy Mass was served by the Cardinal of Lithuania, and a great procession went to the square of the historical museum, where the statue was re-established on the same place as before."

The address by the Cardinal to the people was very political, explicitly claiming independence. They then began to prepare to have democratic elections to the previously powerless Soviet Lithuanian Parliament; "With a choice, with competing ideologies, with competing problems. And there were only two sides then—Communist party or local administration, and Sajudis movement." The 11th March was set as the date for the vote on independence, and on that date the first main issue was the election of the post of President or Chairman of Parliament. The competition was between Landsbergis, as Chairman of Sajudis and the First Secretary of the Communist Party in Lithuania. Landsbergis won "more than two-thirds of the votes" and the position "was the highest authority in the country or head of state" according to the new Constitution.

Landsbergis talked of the "spirit of the people" in Lithuania. On the 13th January 1991, "Soviet tanks and KGB killers went to kill unarmed people in the crowds surrounding TV facilities and Parliament...there was bloodshed. Soviets began to shoot the people, to crush them by tanks. But the spirit was not crushed, the spirit was very strong of those people there. Then there were moments which people remember, and remember that some higher blessing was on us." Landsbergis saw that the people there "were ready to die—it was the same as a spirit of armed resistance. This time people were not armed, only in spirit. Armed resistance was also a movement of free men, making choice to die being free...this feeling of dignity, feeling of necessity to live in the truth, not in a lie... I guess it's coming from Providence, from a higher authority...there were priests serving holy services all night before and after this bloodshed. One of the young priests also was in gulags before." Since that time in 1988 when he walked up the steps and crossed himself before becoming president of Sajudis he has felt some need for this higher authority's strength. "We more and more often attended the holy services. In the open air there were prayers at the beginning of the rallies. We invited priests, especially those active in public life and experienced in gulags and in torturing chambers of KGB, those who worked in underground with Chronicle of the Lithuanian Catholic Church." Landsbergis found the stories of the lives of these priests, who spent time in gulags because of their faith, "remarkable...When they were accused, they 'violated the law,' which forbids the catechisation of children. Some of them used to say: 'We have Jesus' law, which is right. We obey Jesus law.' It was the best example." Though not a heartfelt believer, Landsbergis felt it important to have his children baptised. He explained in some situations he still relies on this 'higher authority'. He went on to tell me that "I always find a very deep wisdom when I am listening to [the gospel] during church services. Sometimes I note it for myself and remember it on paper, and it is the deepest wisdom, brought by Jesus to mankind."

Having discussed with Ulrich Miesel, Tunne Kelam, Maat Laar and Vytautes Landsbergis at length the situations they all experienced it's interesting to note that all four stress the striving for truth and Tunne Kelam's comment that "it's truth that makes you free" really hits home. Truth is not always an easy option for politicians. Too often it's easier to be economical with the truth, or put a spin on situations or simply act dumb. Of course, I would never admit to such practices, no politician ever would. Although I do know one prominent politician who, having distorted the truth, can then firmly believe what he has just said. The Soviet system was based on lies and democracy flourishes when societies are open. Wouldn't it be nice if the electorate actually believed that their representatives were honourable, honest and trustworthy. How to get to that stage would need a book in its own right. As I always say people get the politicians they deserve; if apathy is king then don't be surprised at the outcome.

In the meantime just thank God that there were, and are, people like Ulrich, Tunne, Maat and Vytautes involved in politics.

★ ★ ★ ★

On the 26th February, 2004 I heard the news of a plane disappearing on a flight from Macedonia to Bosnia. One of the passengers was Macedonian President Boris Trajkovski. I had first met him as I interviewed him after he had addressed the Annual Prayer Breakfast in Brussels. I met him on several occasions after, including one time in Washington when we both attended the National Prayer Breakfast there. I considered him to be a friend and he always welcomed me with "Terry, my brother."

His death was a tragic loss not only for his country, but for the Balkan region as a whole. He was driven by his faith and one thing he did want to do was to establish a network of national leaders of faith who could meet regularly to encourage and strengthen one another. The following is, first of all, an extract from The Times obituary column following his death and then an account of our first discussion:

"Boris Trajkovski, Macedonian statesman who strove to preserve the integrity of his country amid the ceaseless conflicts of life in the Balkans

"Boris Trajkovski, who had been President of Macedonia since 1999, had worked tirelessly and bravely for peace and ethnic harmony in his former Yugoslav republic. He almost single-handedly prevented the tiny Balkan nation veering into a full-blown civil war when fighting broke out between ethnic Albanian Guerrillas and Macedonian security forces in 2001.

"Trajkovski first rose to prominence in Balkan politics during the Nato bombing of the rump Yugoslavia in 1999, which was launched in response to a crackdown by Serb forces on ethnic Albanian civilians in the province of Kosovo adjoining the young Macedonian republic. This had obtained its independence from the regime of Slobodan Milosevic, then Yugoslav President, eight years earlier.

"Hundreds of thousands of ethnic Albanians fled from Kosovo, confronting the authorities in Skopje, the Macedonian capital, with a major humanitarian crisis that also threatened to upset the delicate ethnic balance in Macedonia, where some 25 per cent of the population are ethnic Albanians.

"At first, Slavonic hardliners in the ethnic Macedonian community called for the refugees to be refused entry or expelled to other countries. At one stage the Macedonian Government asked the international community to provide it with aircraft to fly refugees out, but Trajkovski, then Deputy Foreign Minister, argued that the refugees should be allowed in and Nato troops hurriedly set about helping relief agencies to house them in camps quickly constructed on Macedonian territory.

"The ethnic Albanian community in Macedonia rewarded Trajkovski's humanity during the Kosovo crisis. When he ran for the Presidency as an underdog candidate in 1999 they voted heavily for him, as did many members of other minorities such as the Turks, Roma, Vlachs, Pomaks and Bosniaks who make up the extraordinary heterogeneous ethnic mix of the modern Macedonian state.

"Although he was a member of the traditionally nationalist Macedonian Internal Revolutionary Organisation (VRMO-DPME), a party with historic links to the Macedonian terrorists who had assassinated King Alexander I of Yugoslavia in Marseilles in 1934, Trajkovski was always on the moderate wing of the modern grouping. He always emphasised the Christian aspect of the Macedonian Christians' struggle for independence from the Ottoman Empire in the 19th century, the period that had spawned the party's forerunner.

"A Methodist lay preacher and professional lawyer, Boris Trajkovski was born in Strumca in 1956. He graduated in jurisprudence from Skopje University in 1980 before completing his education in the United States.

"He joined the VRMO in 1992 at a time when the founding father of the country, President Kiro Gligorov, was struggling to keep Macedonians out of the wars raging in Croatia and Bosnia-Herzegovina, and to overcome deep-seated hostility from Greece, where nationalists claim ancient Macedonia as a part of Hellas. Traditionally, Macedonians feel that their land-locked country is threatened politically by one or more of the so-called 'Four Wolves' surrounding them: Bulgaria, Serbia, Albania and Greece.

"As President, Trajkovski received Western support, essential in a country depending heavily on American and EU aid, he steered Macedonians towards joining Nato and the European Union. The county's position as a crossroads on the old trade route from Turkey to the Aegean and from Serbia to Greece means that the Macedonians have always been convinced that they can attain prosperity so long as they avoid the violent fate of the other former Yugoslav republics.

"By March 2001, however, Trajkovski was under increasing pressure from hardliners in his own party, who wanted the security forces to crack down on ethnic guerrillas. These were known to be planning a guerrilla uprising, led by former members of the Kosovo Liberation Army, to demand greater rights for the ethnic Albanians in education, the army and police. They also wanted Albanian to be recognised as an official language.

"Macedonian special forces troops attacked ethnic Albanian fighters on the border with Kosovo, an act which prompted Ali Ahmeti, the political leader of the newly formed ethnic Albanian National Liberation Army, to set off the uprising earlier than he had planned. Within days the rebels were besieging Tetove, Macedonia's second city, which like much of western Macedonia has an ethnic Albanian minority.

"In the subsequent fighting some 250 people were killed and up to 750 others were wounded, while tens of thousands of refugees left Macedonia. Trajkovski presided over the formation in May 2001 of a grand coalition of national unity which included the opposition Social Democrats as well as his own party and the two main ethnic Albanian parties, to prevent full-scale civil war developing.

"By June, with the help of the international community, he had devised a wide-ranging peace plan—a kind of blueprint for the future of his country— and talks between ethnic Albanian and ethnic Macedonian leaders began on the shores of Lake Ohrid.

"Officials in both Brussels and Nato were determined that international intervention to prevent internecine destruction should not be delayed, as it had been in Croatia and Bosnia-Herzegovina with tragic consequences. Trajkovski was supported by a handful of advisors, but he also received strong personal support from the EU chief foreign envoy, Javier Solana, and the Nato Secretary-General of the day, Lord Robertson of Port Ellen, both of whom visited Skopje several times during the extended crisis. Macedonia's security forces were unable to defeat the more mobile guerrillas, who seized the Skopje suburb of Aracinovo by June 2001 and threatened to shell the international airport and government buildings in the capital.

"Although under intense pressure, Trajkovski remained calm and collected, and with the help of the American and European Union special envoys, James Pardew and François Léotard he arranged for all the parties to sign the so-called Ohrid peace agreement on August 13, 2001.

"At one stage it seemed as if he might be overthrown by Macedonian hardline elements in the Interior Ministry, as an angry mob, irate that ethnic Albanian guerrillas had been escorted out of Aracinova by US peacekeeping troops, stormed part of the presidential palace in Skopje behind the parliament building, many armed with automatic weapons and firing into the air.

"Trajkovski responded with a typically conciliatory speech to the nation, and the hardliners backed down as thousands of British-led Nato peacekeepers were deployed in Macedonia.

"These presided over an arms collection operation in which the guerrillas laid down their weapons in return for recognition of greater rights for ethnic Albanians in education and the right for Albanian MPs to use their own language in parliament.

"By September 2001 the situation had been stabilised. There was little doubt in the minds of Western observers in Skopje during the crisis that Trajkovski, by his courage and force of character, had prevented a fifth Balkan war that might have dragged in Bulgaria and Albania, and possibly even led to hostilities between two Nato members, Greece and Turkey.

"Trajkovski presided patiently over the implementation of the Ohrid agreement's concession to the ethnic Albanians, but after his Herculean efforts he may have been privately happy when he was not selected by his party to run for another term as head of state in the presidential elections expected to be held later this year. His untimely death is likely to revive instability in Macedonia at a time when a recent nationalist resurgence in Serbia has raised fears that ethnic Albanian militants in Kosovo may again try to stir up discontent in Macedonia, as a way to put pressure on the international community to give Kosovo independence from Belgrade.

"Trajkovski is survived by his wife, a son and a daughter."

So from the public description to a personal account.

He told me how his father had been persecuted and imprisoned under the Tito regime, "partly because of his Protestant religious beliefs but partly because he was opposing of the Communist regime." He was sentenced to hard labour at the site of Tito's villa; having "no idea that his soon to be born son would one day be the President residing in the same villa." When he was a child there were many difficulties associated with being a practising Christian. "With my Law Degree that I did at the Law School I was not able to get a job because I was a Christian, because I had been very active. For 12 years I had been with the President of the Methodist Church in Yugoslavia. Before the dissolution of Yugoslavia I was leading youth work for 12 years. It was very difficult even in the newspapers. We couldn't imagine a Methodist leader who is a lawyer partly because the law education is based on the Communist practising of the law." In a speech given at the European Parliament Prayer Breakfast, Boris remarked, "Truly, God works in mysterious ways. How did the son of a tractor driver…who was a member of a Methodist community in an atheist state become President? Though I could tell you the events that led to my Presidency, I cannot tell you why the hand of God worked the way it did. But I am very thankful for His love and mercy and for the privilege of serving Him in the role of President of the Republic of Macedonia."

Boris does not baulk at talking publicly about his faith in Macedonia. He explained that the press react very negatively, often making fun of him. The opening remarks in his speeches addressing the country or the Parliament usually contain biblical quotations and a call for God's help. He believes very strongly in a need for "Christian principles to lead us in creating prosperity" and stresses the importance of "the process of reconciliation, the process of forgiveness, the process of repentance and afterwards the healing process using examples and principles based on the Bible." In reaction to such an overt Christian message he told me, "half of the people are very supportive but there is no related culture, people are not expecting that the President will draw them with such kind of message." He talks of the need to base leadership on "eternal and absolute principles, not what is popular opinion; the nature of politics is…to get re-elected at all cost. I cannot express how strong of a temptation this is. I cannot let public opinion sway me from doing what I believe to be right and moral. I must lead the people based on God's eternal principles of justice and mercy." He explained that, "integrity and honesty defined Jesus' leadership," and that although "misleading the public avoids immediate political damage, there is always a backlash as people loose respect for political leaders…Honesty is always the best policy." He told me that Chris Patten, "is very honest with me, he said 'because you are a very honest person, everything we ask to you, you did it. Because of you we want to help.'"

Boris described the events leading up to the writing of the preamble of the Macedonian constitution. Whilst waiting for Javier Solana in his office he told me, "I was reading strongly my favourite verse and also my favourite psalms, 25, 23, 41 and when he [Solana] arrived he was very frustrated. He submit me one paper…before it arrived I said, 'no weapon forged against me will prevail' and he arrived in my office…and said 'I am submitting to you this paper… take it or leave it'." Trajkovski told him, " 'It is not possible for me to accept this' …and I try to change something in the text. All of a sudden he left the room and I was very calm…and after five or ten minutes my protocol people said Mr. Solana would like to see you, he is begging to come back…he is going back and forth, back and forth with other parties and I was waiting for his final decision and he called me through the phone and he said, 'Boris, we succeeded we succeeded!' And I said 'Praise to God! Let me now explain to you why this happen'." Trajkovski saw God working through him for the Macedonian people. The situation appeared intransigent, but he trusted in God, remained calm and an agreement was reached. However, neither Solana nor the Prime Minister were able to see the "miracle."

Boris told me he believes when a country is "led by a real believer," be that the Head of State or Government that "blessings will earlier or later arrive." He told me his region has experienced God's blessing, and explained that it would be very easy for a President who was not a Christian to unthinkingly use the military to solve problems, whereas "a Christian asks God what is wise," and knows that God is everywhere and is ultimately in control. In reaction to accusations that religion is the cause of many problems, he explained, "This is only part of the evil; it is not the different denominations causing the problems, more obviously in ex-Yugoslavian Republic, it is the politics." He told me his faith helps him to "better understand the needs of my people… their frustrations. My faith in Jesus makes me strong to love enemies. It also makes me strong to show to the people that beside our differences we have to live together and work together, to respect each other, regardless of our division among ourselves." Boris also believes that leaders should be servants. He follows Jesus' call for those who want to be first to make themselves the very last, and to be the servant of all. In his speech he said, "A true leader lives for a higher cause. An empty life consists of living for self; a full and rich self consists of serving others." Boris used the example of Jesus when he contemplated the death that was awaiting him; though he wished for his suffering to end, he "humbly submitted to God's plan…It was not his will, but God's." Boris prays "all the time". When questioned as to whether God ever says "no" to his requests, he told me "Sometimes His plans are not my plans and His will is not my will." Therefore God's answer might be, " 'not now, but later', in accord with His plans."

He was a wonderful, humble man, whose legacy will live on for the benefit of his people and country. The European Parliament's specialist in the region, Doris Pack, attended the funeral. She knew of my connections with Boris and came to me and said "His death united the country as all the different ethnic groupings gathered in their thousands. Even in death he was reconciling that country."

The beauty of my job is that I get to meet and befriend such people. I learn from them and hopefully can use their experiences and lives to reflect how faith can fit into politics and what a difference it can make. It does beg the question that if he was such a force for good in that region, then why did he have to die the way he did? All part of God's plan? God putting you where He thinks you should be? Or simply that it's not God's role to tamper with the mechanisms of an aircraft that may have been faulty and it's certainly not His job to alter the force of gravity so that the plane wouldn't crash.

So from the testimonies of those who survived the Cold War and Communist dictatorship, the next two chapters reflect on two survivors of the apartheid regime.

If Jim Wallis asks "Where are the prophets today?" then look no further.

FOUR

I fell in love with South Africa the moment I saw Table Mountain for the first time. I was a twenty one year-old fourth engineer on the SS Manaar. The shipping company that I worked for Thos. and Jno. Brocklebank Ltd didn't normally do the Cape, but thanks to the Six Day War the Suez Canal was closed and shippers who carried cargo to Asia made the most of the long detour by getting business where they could. This was 1968 and as we docked in Cape Town I was met by my dad's brother who had been stationed in South Africa during World War II, married a local girl and never returned to the UK. We drove up to Port Elizabeth where they lived, spent the weekend there, then I flew up to Durban to rejoin the ship.

South Africa is God's own country. Unfortunately, at that time and since the end of World War II, the apartheid policies of the Nationalist Party were well entrenched. Much as I loved the place, I couldn't have lived there under that system.

Since being an MEP, I've had many opportunities to visit there on a regular basis, making many friends and seeing how the EU helped in the transformation of the country. During the apartheid years the Special Programme from the EU helped fund NGOs for education, training, and job creation, channelled through the churches, the trade unions and the Kagiso Trust. The EU was the single biggest donor to the people of South Africa during those apartheid years, helping the very people that the Nationalist Government would not help. One of the people who helped negotiate the Special Programme in the eighties was Father Smangaliso Mkhatshwa, who became an MP in the first ANC government of 1994 and is now Mayor of greater Pretoria or Tshwane, to give it its proper title. When I visited him shortly after the 1994 elections, he pointed out that previously the white Nationalist Party MPs had been predominantly a rubber stamp for the government and consequently had few facilities. He pointed out that there were now 60 MPs on his floor in the Parliament building with one typist to do their work. At the same time Gill Marcus MP, who was then Chair of the Finance Committee, explained how if she wanted a report to be given to members of her committee, then she had to get the paper, type it out, photocopy it and distribute it to the members. I went back to Brussels and put pressure on the Commission to make sure this new-found democracy could work by making sure we trained MPs and to ensure they had the means to do their work. Shortly after, an EU funded programme channelled through the Speaker's Office, began to do just that, not only for the MPs, but also for those members of the Provincial Legislatures. I like to think I played a small part in making this happen.

What was obvious after several visits was that the transition from apartheid to democracy had not been the bloodbath that many were predicting for an obvious reason. It had come about because so many who had suffered under apartheid were prepared to forgive and many had been taught forgiveness through their faith. The churches in the townships, the Christian Institute, the South African Council of Churches, dedicated ordained and lay people had all played a significant part in The Struggle. The irony being that the apartheid system had been underpinned by the Dutch Reform Church. But great Christians from that church, like Beyers Naudé, were prepared to speak out against this evil.

In South Africa I have seen some of the worst poverty and abysmal living conditions that one could have the misfortune to see. Yet within the townships and adjoining shanty towns, people can still demonstrate their faith. People who have felt the burden of apartheid can still give thanks to God for what little they have. They are grateful for each small mercy. When you have no access to fresh water, no sanitation, no electricity, then life takes on a whole different meaning compared to those of us who take such things for granted and don't think twice about the consequences of not having them.

This was demonstrated to me by a group of people who eeked out a living by working a rubbish dump i.e. salvaging cans and bottles. When I met them, they were spotless, the white shirts gleaning and the patterned dresses looking wonderful. They themselves had named the dump Las Vegas and were being helped by Mercy Clinic, run by the Sisters of Mercy in Winterveld. If you look for Winterveld on a map of South Africa you'll be lucky to find it and if you do, it will be no more than a pin-prick. It's where the apartheid regime forced those people that were turfed off their land to go to their new homeland in Bophuthatswana, all one million of them. It's a desolate place with no work and little hope. Yet in the midst of it the EU financed church-based organisations to help in primary health care, the fight against AIDS, training and education. I was there to assess what was being done. I met some remarkable people, real living Saints who had dedicated themselves to working with the people there. At one clinic run by the Catholic Church, because of AIDS they encouraged the use of condoms and distributed them free. When I was about to ask the obvious question, I was told, "We see them as protection, not contraception." At an Anglican centre the nurse and her doctor husband had had their house raided by youths who tied them all up and luckily only robbed them. The same gang raped one of their health visitors and murdered a man the next day. But they wouldn't leave, they are committed to their work. "Why do you stay?" I asked. "Because I am a Christian and this is where God wants me to be," the woman said. I saw so many ordinary people who are doing extra-ordinary tasks like trying to empower other women in their daily lives. But if Winterveld was bad, then Khayelitsha on the Cape Flats was hell on earth. Once again a million people living in abject squalor in the murder capital of South Africa. At a disused cement works the offices had been taken over by another church-based organisation funded by the EU. It was run by a Canadian. When I gave him my card 'Terry Wynn MEP for Merseyside East and Wigan', he said, "and how's Wigan and St Helens rugby league teams." This was unreal, in the middle of the cess-pit, where human beings have to live, I'm taking about Rugby League.

The doctor and wife team story has an interesting twist to it. They could easily have commuted the 40 km to Pretoria each day, but instead chose to live in a breeze-block building they called home with their two children, one of whom was an adopted African with a disability of the legs. She said that her Christianity had been influenced by the trial of a group of white South Africans who were conscientious objectors and would not join the South African armed forces. "The judge said to one of them that you call yourself a Christian, well in Romans chapter 13 vs 1 it says you should *obey* the authorities, so why are you not obeying the law of the land," she continued, "To which he replied, with the greatest respect your honour, the word that St. Paul used in the original Greek was 'whatever', but he knew it, then he says, which means to *submit* to the authorities. Now I am prepared to submit to your judgement, but not obey a law that says I must kill fellow South Africans. It really hit home to me that their faith could mean so much and I've tried to live my life as a Christian since then."

When I arrived in Cape Town, Robert de Vogleare, who worked for the EU

Delegation in South Africa and was my minder on this trip, was taking me to the various projects. He kept suggesting we visit a project named TEFSA. I kept insisting we didn't have time, but he was persistent and said we really should, so I said okay, but only for 10 minutes. The CEO was Roy Jackson and in my notes from then I have it down as "brilliant meeting." During the conversation, Roy Jackson said something like:

"When I was in prison,"
"What for?" I asked.
"I was a conscientious objector," he replied.
"Has this anything to do with Romans 13 vs 1?"
"How did you know that?" he said.

Small world isn't it.

But of all the people I have befriended in South Africa, there is one that stands out from all the rest, Cedric Mayson, who I wrote about in Onward Christian Socialist. There I discussed his time in prison and the torture he had and it's hard to appreciate the amount of forgiveness one person can have. To quote two small passages from his book *A Certain Sound*: *5am Cronwright and nine others at the door. Fifteen months in detention awaiting trial, months of it locked in solitary confinement for twenty-three hours out of twenty-four, ... Arthur Benoni Cronwright. For nearly a decade this man sat at his desk in the Security Police Offices on the tenth floor of John Vorster Square in Johannesburg, fingering the men and women who bugged our phones, read our mail, watched our houses, followed our cars, plagued our families, infiltrated our meetings, issued our banning orders, detained, arrested and tried us-and, in the end, missed me. I hated that little Hitler man with his shrieking fanaticism for a couple of days in 1976, and it took me months to recover. It made me resolve never to hate anyone again; I couldn't stand it.*

The hatred came about after a period of torture. His words have had a profound affect on me and I've come to realise that hatred does nothing to the person you are aiming it at but it certainly does a lot to yourself.

Amidst the poverty of South Africa, in the townships I've witnessed and felt the power of the Holy Spirit more than in any other place. At the beginning of 2003, I realised that it had been two years since I had visited there and felt like a drug addict with withdrawal symptoms. I needed a shot to satisfy my craving so I went and on this occasion Cedric introduced me to one of his friends from the days of The Struggle, Father Albert Nolan.

We met at Cedric's house and Father Nolan explained how he became a priest. "I worked in a bank for four years where I basically watched people crooking other people out of money. If this is the world I was in, I needed to do something about that. I couldn't just sit there and say 'I'm a clerk, I count other people's money.' I decided I really wanted to do something to help people, not just to make money. I realised the gospel, the values that I stood for, had to get into business. It was only later that I recognised that those same values had to get into politics also. That's how I became a Catholic priest and I am a Dominican in the Catholic priesthood. I studied theology and all the rest." He was inspired to get involved in politics through two fields of work. One was working with poor people and seeing their suffering. "It was the days of apartheid, of course, so they were black people, and I saw what was happening to them." He was also a student chaplain in east Cape Town, and became involved in politics through students. "It was the days when politics was the issue for university students, black and white. I became particularly involved in an organisation called 'Young Christian Students'. I worked with both black and white students. The gospel imperative was certainly driving me not to avoid the issues, but to face them head-on and to do what seemed to me to be the right thing in the circumstances. So the gospel was an important factor."

"Some people in the churches thought you don't get involved in politics at all, and that was quite a common opinion in those days. So we had problems." Christians were accused of being, "too involved, or too radical." Many were accused of being Communists and therefore not Christians. "That was quite common in the Catholic church. In 1977 the bishops asked me to do a survey of how the Catholic church coped with socialist governments around the world, because they were already beginning to think that South Africa was going to have a socialist government of some kind. So I did a survey, through the church, not even through the Communist Party, of what was going on—Angola, Mozambique, Vietnam, Cuba, Nicaragua, East Germany... I came to the conclusion that in fact the church coped quite well where it was a socialist government, except where there was a policy of actually persecuting the church, which wasn't necessarily everywhere. Among the people I interviewed the Archbishop of what was Saigon said, 'No, we get on really well with them and we have the same ideals.' So I wrote that up for the bishops. Wow, if I ever became a 'persona non gratis' it was that day, because I said, 'Well, there are lots of things in socialism that are much the same as what we would say as Christians, apart from the fact that any government might persecute the church, whatever its ideology or policy'. As far as policies were concerned, I couldn't see what the problem was. Anyway, most of them didn't like that." His research was never published. "One bishop actually got up and said, 'We must scrap this from the record. It mustn't even be recorded that we tabled it.' "

"I was a member of the ANC, but I don't think the whole of the church knew that. I think it couldn't be public or you'd go to jail straight away. By and large, the church authorities wouldn't have approved, that's certainly true." Father Nolan described the political activities he was involved in. "We had political rallies, talks, protest marches, demonstrations, that kind of activity. And then meetings to plan all these things, how to change the mentality of the church about apartheid, how to mobilise more people into the anti-apartheid movement. I didn't belong to the underground. It was ordinary political activity that you might do anywhere, anytime really, except for us it was special." He explained that priests would not usually have felt it necessary to get involved in politics, but in this context it was necessary. "It wasn't just a political campaign, one political party versus another. This for us was dismantling apartheid, getting rid of an illegitimate government, and you had to get the church in. At least part of the problem was theological, because the apartheid government used theology to justify what it was doing."

The Kairos Document was compiled by Christians fighting against apartheid and addressed the government's use of Christianity to justify the apartheid regime. "Ministers from Soweto said: 'This is a huge crisis for us. What are we going to say in the pulpit? Can we preach Christianity when our children are being killed in the name of Christianity?' Some people did, but if you were honest you couldn't just carry on preaching Christianity while people were doing something like that in its name. The Kairos Document identified three kinds of theology in use. It speaks of state theology, used to justify what the state is doing, in this case apartheid. The second part was called church theology. That was a theology to keep the church as it was, with its privileges, not to upset the upper crust too much, keep some kind of relationship with the state, while it was perhaps a little critical. The third one we called prophetic theology, and that was the kind of theology that, like the prophets of old and Jesus, would speak out about what was wrong, regardless of what's going to happen, regardless of whether the church was going to be persecuted as a result. You spoke the truth. That was the kind of theology we tried to exercise. We saw clearly, then as now, that anyone can use the gospel, Jesus, the church, for their own purposes. We were very clear about the wrongness of what the state was doing."

"The churches had to contradict what the government was saying, to explain that the government's viewpoint was not a Christian one, and that if you opposed the government's theology it did not mean that you were a Communist and therefore an atheist." Father Nolan explained that because the church used theology in such a way, "probably more people got involved in politics in South Africa because of their faith than many other places."

He then spoke about the current relationship between the church, faith and politics. "Many of the leading church people in the struggle are now in government rather than in the church. If you say to me: 'What difference does their faith make?', the thought that comes to mind is: 'They don't have time to think about what difference their faith should make or could make to what they're doing.' It could make a lot of difference if people spent more time thinking about, even reflecting on their faith, let alone how it relates to politics. They don't give enough time to finding their own ways of expressing faith. One has to find a way of living that means God is totally central to one's life. A lot of people have something they call faith, but it's pretty much on the margins. Now, what one's really got to ask is what would happen to me in relation to policies if God was central, if faith was central, if Jesus Christ was really my guide and model and example. Not very many people are in that position. Some are, some aren't. So there are people for whom God is totally central." Cedric interjected to explain that politicians "get caught up in promoting the political policy," and need to take time out to reflect as a group. He added that much of the clergy also "are too busy...they don't think, they don't read, they don't get together to envisage anything. That sort of thing is missing."

We talked about whether Nelson Mandela was a Christian. Father Nolan believes he is, though Mandela does not often mention it. "When he became President he made it quite clear that he wasn't going to stand up as a Methodist or even as a Christian, and to be President of South Africa at that particular time, you had to be open and kind of neutral. What that effectively meant was that you don't express what you believe publicly. That's a crazy situation for anyone to be in. But politically that's what he had to do." In one interview Mandela said he believed in God, but "he was very, very careful about how he expressed it so that it didn't appear to be dividing the society." Father Nolan described one South African priest and politician, as thinking, "first and foremost like a politician...I can't imagine him standing up one day and saying: 'No, I can't accept what the party's saying', because of his faith. I don't think he's going to upset the political apple cart in the name of faith."

Father Nolan is disappointed that the church is now less involved in politics. "Many church people who had been involved in The Struggle said, 'Now we go back to the church. We don't worry about society and social things, well, not much anyway'. The fundamentalists had been saying: 'No, we don't get involved in politics. It's nothing to do with us.' When they had a new government, suddenly they said: 'You do get involved in politics' and were protesting about the government, mainly because it was a black government. Also because it wasn't a government that forwarded or gave privileges to Christianity, which of course apartheid did." We then discussed the relationship between Christianity and Western culture. "I think the Christian faith has influenced even highly secularised Europe in a lot of ways. There's a history behind it that means there are certain values that wouldn't have been there without Christianity, an indirect influence."

He then went on to talk of the present situation. "The materialist world we live in, where money and power and all the rest are much more important than anything spiritual, is getting a kind of backlash and you get a 'hunger for spirituality', which I analyse as people feeling they don't have inner peace in themselves, or they feel they don't have inner strength. The limitations of the materialist way of life are being recognised. Something spiritual is needed, inner peace, inner strength, some meaning in life, something to hope for, something beyond ourselves. That feeling is growing. That's very important because faith is precisely the answer to that. It's food for that kind of hunger." Father Nolan pointed out that is why more and more people are interested in activities such as yoga and the New Age. He then talked about the limitations of science. "The scientists are getting there very fast with 'We don't know'. When they start going deeper and deeper into the molecule and the atom they are at a point where they say they don't know. When they go looking up to the ever-expanding universe, with a billion galaxies and a billion stars in a galaxy...It's totally mysterious."

"The mystery of life and the mystery of God is far beyond all of us. We have to see that there are billions of years to come and that we have a long way to develop and it's not as if one can feel that faith ought to play a big role here and now, next year or something like that, but we're in the middle of something, we're in the middle of faith having played an important role, but faith having to be purified, having to be changed, having to be adapted; consciousness generally having to be deepened. Some of that is happening and we live at a time where those changes are happening. We don't live at a time where we were kind of stuck and just carrying on as before, and that's quite exciting, but there's a long way to go. One can open one's mind to all sorts of possibilities like, I mean, the human race may not continue, we may destroy the earth and therefore destroy ourselves, but that's not the end at all."

"I think we're going through a very important stage of Christianity. Christianity has been just a cultural phenomenon for a lot of people. It's Western culture. If you were Western, you grew up as a Christian and didn't really make the choice, you just took it for granted." Father Nolan talked of how the Reformers of the past such as Wesley were trying to get people to choose to be Christians and then to commit to following Jesus, not just to be a Christian because of their culture. He explained "People will be Christians really and truly by choice, certainly not because everyone else is. Against the odds sometimes, certainly not just following the crowd." At the moment he sees Christianity being sidelined. "Some people wouldn't dream of calling themselves Christians and when they meet someone who's a Christian, they say: 'Mad! Do you still go to church? What's wrong with you?' All of that is not necessarily a bad thing. It's a purging. People are taking responsibility for what they believe or don't believe, and people are asking questions, and that's important too." He believes that through this process Christians will increasingly have a more genuine and deeper faith, and that faith will play an increasingly important role in society as spiritual hunger increases.

Even though South Africa is becoming more Westernised, Cedric explained, "We are unusual in comparison with Europe because the churches on the whole are still full, and the churches in the townships are packed, bursting their seams. Even more so than I remember in the past. I think for some people the church and going to church on Sunday has become the new culture, replacing the old, traditional African culture perhaps. It's become the way of being a community for many people: 'This is my community, this is where I belong, this is where I do good things, this is where I feel good and give meaning to my life.' Their faith is not particularly deep in that sense, but I mean, there's a reality there, there's a definite reality there. The church is a community building institution for black people. Even when it is dreadful at times, and the sermons are terrible, and all that kind of thing, and the kind of Christianity being pushed makes you want to squirm perhaps at times."

He makes the comparison with his experience with the Southern Baptists in the United States. "That was a really amazing experience because they spent the whole service building community, and different people in church would come up and say what they were doing, what they wanted to do, and getting others involved in doing it. There was a picnic and they would tell everybody who would come to the picnic what happened at the picnic and then there was an autistic child. Everybody knew the family and all the rest. The child was brought up and I think it was the child's birthday. You could see that child felt he belonged somewhere. It was an amazing experience. Someone else had passed exams. That was part of the service. It was just extraordinary how much it bound people together, and that's what it was about."

Father Nolan remarked that in South Africa, "Many of the best theologians of those times are no longer doing theology," and then told me he sees the established church there as failing Christianity. He is at odds with some of their theology. To put forward what he believes to be the gospel message he told me, "There's no one way of doing it. For example, I do it from within the church. I'm involved in the structures of the church, and I'm trying within those limitations to ensure that the priests of today and particularly the priests of tomorrow, the younger people, are going to have a deeper faith, are going to be people who really believe in God and are prayerful people. It's not a big public thing. I give a lot of talks and lectures, in that sense try to influence people. But I keep within the parameters if you like. Another way of doing it is to break out of that and try to speak to people. The problem of being outside of [the church] is that you need some kind of context, credibility, platform, otherwise you can totally sideline yourself so that you don't have an audience anymore. Maybe you can write a book and hope that people will read it, but each one of us has to find a way of developing our own faith but also influencing others. To pass on something of your own experience and yet give them the freedom to develop it in their way. As you get older, you think about how younger people are going to come up and take that over. It's not changing the world immediately, but it's sowing seeds. That's what one must do, and that's what I have to go back and do."

It's amazing how he talks of prophetic theology "the kind of theology like the prophets of old and Jesus would speak out about what was wrong," in the same way that Jim Wallis does. Or the way he sees the problems of a materialist world in the same way that Ulrich Miesel does. But the comment I find most interesting and one to focus the mind is when he says "… there are billions of years to come and we have to develop…. The human race may not continue, we may destroy the earth and therefore destroy ourselves, but that's not the end at all."

Now that's what I call faith in an almighty, omnipotent, eternal God, that recognises that this life is indeed a mere pin-prick in eternity.

FIVE

Those who have been bitten by the bug of Africa will know what I mean when I say that it gets into your blood and draws you back time and time again. Africa is such a fascinating place with wonderful people and, as I said in Chapter 4, it's there that I have felt, more than anywhere else, the presence of the Holy Spirit and seen it in a variety of individuals, on societies, in townships, through speeches and music, through dedication and humility. No wonder Ubuntu is an African word (explained later).

Originally the idea was to do this book with Cedric Mayson, a person who has, as you may have gathered, influenced me immensely.

I first met him, and his wife Penelope, in February 1993 when I was attending an ANC Conference in South Africa being held in Johannesburg. It was quite an historic occasion and it concluded with a service in the Catholic Church of Regina Mundi in the heart of Soweto. It was one of the most emotional, spiritual experiences of my life, one that I'll never forget. I was sat with British MPs Joan Lester and Bob Hughes, the then Chairman of the Anti-Apartheid Movement. Bob turned to me at the end and said, "As an atheist, even I was moved by that." Cedric had organized it and a month later, I was back with Doris my wife and our friendship grew from then.

I had known of him before. In 1953 as a young, fresh Methodist minister he was influenced by that great Methodist Dr. W. E. Sangster to go to South Africa. After the Sharpville massacre his activities in the struggle against apartheid increased. The then regime had an instrument of "banning" people, that is putting them under house arrest and only allowing them to meet one person at a time.

Cedric was banned, then he was imprisoned, spent time in solitary, was tortured then put on trial.

He escaped from the country in 1983 living in exile until he and his family returned nine years later. He tells of the neighbour who had looked after his car all those years and of going into his local Italian restaurant for the first time in nine years to be greeted with the words "your usual table Mr and Mrs Mayson."

He is a remarkable character with a wonderful sense of humour. My wife says that there is an aura about him that radiates goodness, to which he would laugh if you ever said that to him.

When he did get involved in the struggle the Church dropped him like a ton of bricks. He worked for the South African Council of Churches and the Christian Institute with Beyers Naude. Thanks to having no pension from the Methodist Church he is still working, well into his seventies, and heads the Commission for Religious Affairs within the African National Congress. He is passionate in his beliefs, doesn't like New Labour, Tony Blair or George Bush. It is always a pleasure to be in his company and the fact that we didn't do the book together is a disappointment. However, this chapter will be his contribution and will show how having a "soul" matters.

This first part of the chapter contains some extracts of his thoughts, which he shared with a variety of people, including me. They are taken from "Exploring Spiritual Socialism" (good socialist that he is), a paper that he is working on.

As we reflect on our past, our future, and our present we are conscious of a spiritual drive within us, whether we are religious or not. It is fed by our traditions and imported religions, but is essentially an experience of South African spirituality today. God did not create us and then move to outer space, but is part of the process. God is not outside existence but the very nature of it. Dr. J. Seoka writes: "African spirituality is antecendent to, and the corollary of biblical mythology ... the African people were believers in **Umvelingangi,** *the ONE whose appearance is unknown; the Ancient of Days,* **Unkulunkulu;** *The Great one,* **Modimo;** *the one who penetrates and permeates all being,* **Mothlhodi,** *the source of being. When Paul said, 'God was in Christ' and 'Christ is in you' he was saying the same thing, but modern Christians often find it difficult to update the context."*

We sense both the physical aspect of existence from stars to stomach aches and also the spiritual aspects of reality. We are conscious of being-ness. We are not only driven by the pressures of hunger and thirst and violence, but by the energies of faith, hope and love. All religions and many secular philosophies agree that the heart of the spiritual life of humans is a collective caring for one another. Humanity will only work by love, existence is preserved by love; (Love = joy, peace, patience, kindness, generosity, loyalty, humility and self-control, according to Paul.)

Darwin concluded that physical development happened through the survival of the fittest, but the spiritual development of the human community happens by collective concern for the survival of the weakest: by love. That is the way it is and the way it progresses. The world will not work any other way. This spiritual nature of existence has led all peoples to forms of religion. Asserting that something is religious—music, architecture or politics—means celebrating this spirituality. Spirituality is not a religious invention but an attribute of all human beings, like self, sex and the herd/community. Atheists and agnostics reject religion, but they are deeply spiritual beings like everyone else. It is this spiritual reality of loving and caring for all, including the weakest which produces the concept of democratic government and a just, shared economy. Like the law of gravity, the Ruling Power of God (RPG) is the way things are. If we get it right, spiritual socialism is not a political choice but a rediscovery of the only successful path of life for the human community. If we get it right.

The equation of spiritual with religion, like the equation of economics with capitalism, has been a major disaster for the world. It is the Good News about what God is doing in us, not what we must do for God. Humanity cannot work under divisive, self-centred, power-hungry, religious institutions, or greed-based, self-centred, power-hungry economic structures (both of which think they alone are the way of God) Such forms of society may exercise oppressive control for a while, like fascism or apartheid, but have no future, and must be replaced. In the years of Apartheid we knew that the 'system' was wrong and could not survive, and we also knew that we must spell out an alternative vision focussed in the "Freedom Charter" and struggle for it.

African concepts of life are holistic and appreciate the unity of spirituality and politico-economics in the human community. Faith and politics are two sides of the same coin. Godliness in life exerts a bias against bad and for good. Spirit and material must be considered together. Individual and community practise an essential linkage. The concepts of 'motho ke Modimo' expresses the mystery that the human is a good portion, a tributary of the Supreme Vital Force (Modimo) itself. This is ignored in human relationships at great peril to those who do so.

At the heart of human society is the transforming power of God; love as a hard political, economic, social and theological reality. The RPG is a liberating spiritual power driving the material process. 'Not by might and not by power but by my spirit,' says Yahweh Sabaoth. The engine of power at the ground of our being is love; love with nails in its palms.

Competitive religious industries have nurtured the belief that 'we' are right and 'they' are wrong. Fundamentalists condemn everyone except themselves. Such conflicts are not between the founders and inspirers of religions, but from the institutions of their followers (who have other economic and political agendas). In proclaiming the RPG, Jesus is talking the same language as the Hebrew Bible and the Qur'an, the Hindu ways to salvation, the Buddhist Eight-fold path, the pursuits of Lao Tze, many other philosophers, and African traditional religion.

"The African has a sense of the wholeness of life," writes Canon Luke Pato. "In traditional African religion there is no separate community of religious people because everyone who participates in the life of the community participates also in its religion."

"The African world view rejects popular dichotomies between the sacred and the secular, the material and the spiritual. All life is sacred, all life is of a piece," says Archbishop Tutu.

Each approach is formulating the foundational inspiration of the human community, and their similarities are far more than their differences. The same 'faith experience' drives them all. It is when the institutions depart from the inspiration that they divide us.

Many Christians have stumbled over the words of Jesus in John 14.6: 'I am the Way, the Truth and the Life, no one can come to the Father except through me.' They have interpreted this to mean that other religions are invalid. Yet only four versus earlier Jesus says: 'In my Father's house are many rooms' which embraces the universalist approach of the whole Bible. In fact, there is no problem here, as Harvey Cox (amongst many others) has pointed out.

> "This curious juxtaposition of seemingly contradictory texts ...is telling us about the need to hold the universal and the particular together, and about the central place Jesus must have for

Christians even in the most expansive inter-faith dialogue."

Muslims, Hindus, Jews and African traditionalists could say exactly the same thing. We have our own insights: but we walk on two legs.

For many decades South Africans 'believed in the struggle'. Liberation from apartheid was coming: that faith drove us on expressing the life force within us. We might expound it in terms of Jesus or the Prophet, align it with the story of the Exodus, illustrate it from the sagas of the East or the injunctions of our ancestors who spoke to us in dreams, but these explanations only underwrite the experience. Because of this vital force of faith within us we could sing 'We shall overcome', pray Nkosi sikelel'i Africa', and dance.

Throughout the long difficult history of religion, at the heart of all the struggles against oppression and heresy, it is the constant emergence of faith in the RPG which has given people vision and energy. The essential task of religious socialists is to be proclaimers of the vision and the energy of faith (not to become politicians or economists, though they may be that too).

The Nguni word 'ubuntu' is rapidly becoming a part of the English language like, khaki, lingua franca, or viva. 'Ubuntu ngumuntu ngabantu' means a person is a person through other persons. It is an attitude not an intellectual theory.

"Ubuntu is an African understanding of humanity. Ubuntu means living as a complete human being. It has to do with realising one's full potential as a person. This is an affirmation of a way of life that embodies the qualities of decency, honesty, integrity, and a respect for others." (Stanley Mogoba).

"Africans recognise life as life-in-community. We can truly know ourselves if we remain true to our community, past and present. The concept of individual success or failure is secondary. The ethnic group, village, the locality, are crucial in one's estimation of oneself. Our nature as being-in-relation is a two-way relation: with God and with our fellow human beings." (Mercy Oduyoye 1979)

"Whatever happens to the individual happens to the whole group, and whatever happens to the whole group happens to the individual. The individual can only say "I am, because we are and since we are, I am." (John S Nbiti 1970)

"The most cherished principle in life-together is to include rather than to separate." (Gabriel Setiloane)

Throughout the continent, Africa's triple heritage of Traditional Spirituality, Christianity and Islam affirms the idea of communal being. Prophet Muhammad and his followers are encouraged five times a day to congregate at mosques to worship and to be a mirror to each other. Jesus is a communal knowing: "I am where two or three are met together in my name." Not one on their own; not two or three million: two or three—a commune. And this is the basis of Spiritual Socialism.

The crucial experience of the liberation struggle in South Africa was the ability to believe in it. Oppressed, tortured, imprisoned, with no hope or vision except our own, we had a vivid, living, powerful experience of faith that liberation was on the way and power was in the people. Amandla! Out of that crucible emerged refreshing, prophetic experiences such as the Christian Institute, the SA Council of Churches, Contextual Theology, the Call of Islam, and Jews for Social Justice.

"Many people today are faith-less. Religion is considered irrelevant and is largely misunderstood by many," said Dr. W. E. Sangster who wrote in 1947: "How to get God's order on earth!—there is a problem. And it isn't a problem only of feeble will. It has to be thought out before it can be wrought out. Many Christians haven't seen it yet. Religion, they think, is individual goodness. Wrestling with social and political theories, even though it is undertaken in the name and to the glory of God, seems hardly a spiritual occupation to them. So far from seeing that religion and politics belong at a deep level together, they dread the contact lest it contaminate the things of God."

Many religious people are simply not on God's wavelength. This experience of faith is not belief in a creed or ecclesiastical institution, but the vision and energy inspired by the RPG in our own circumstances. Such faith is often ignored in the US, Europe and the Middle East. It wavers in Africa. And without the driving empowering vision of faith the people perish, the RPG is denied, and we seem to be drifting helplessly at sea in a maelstrom of lostness.

Bede Griffiths, the English monk long resident in India, suggested that behind the breakdown of economic, social and political structures of the present civilisation there has been a reversal of human values, a spiritual break down, which has brought into play forces beyond the material and the human, forces of the unconscious which we cannot control. He sees the only recovery through a rediscovery of the traditional wisdom found in all religions, which themselves have to be renewed so that a new cosmic universal religion can emerge in which the essential values of the Christian religion will be preserved in living relationship with the other religious traditions of the world.

It is this common ground of being that South Africans find as they share and build on the spiritual realities in their own diverse experience.

Clearly, between the deep blue sea and the devil, we have a world-wide problem. Many people who want to play a role are misled by the dictators of capital and fundamentalism, choking to death on materialism, poisoning themselves and their children with the heresies of false religious teaching, and suffering a fatal intellectual indigestion from over-fed, self-indulgent, anti-spiritual individualism which is destroying human community. We have produced a junk generation, stuffed on junk food, junk theologies, and junk objectives.

The Good News of the Ruling Power of God on Earth, spiritual strength and socialism, a transformed world—this is the vision of spiritual socialism empowered by faith. We need to review the basis of our faith and preach it loud and clear with its full ecumenical (inter-faith) and political dimensions.

"Communities of faith have far more in common than the things that divide them," says Bishop Buti Thlagale. "We should meet regularly with the participation of people of all faiths to promote Salaam, Shanti, peace, ukuthula," writes Shishupal Rambharos. It needs the insights and pressures of the primal religious experience focussed in African Indigenous Church and Traditional Spirituality. Spiritual Socialists need to consult on the scope of sanctity, and the Islamic cosmology of the lower self and how it veils the divine spirit within. The software for our computers, so to speak, is imperative to drive the RPG.

People have to be changed to leave both their religious bunkers and their agnostic bunkers if the world is to be transformed.

Rev. Frank Chikane, formerly leader of the SA Council of Churches and now heading President Thabo Mbeki's office, puts one aspect:

"Religious institutions need to accompany the process of reconstruction and rebuilding of a new society through the stages of defining vision about the issues we must deal with, and involvement in the formulation of policy perspectives. This requires a capacity to analyse and make an intelligent contribution. We must not allow ourselves to be reduced to traditional debates concerning homosexuality, abortion and the like ... but engage with the government on a reconstruction of the totality of society."

Rev. Mvume Dandala, newly appointed General Secretary of the All Africa Council of Churches, sets out another aspect:

"We require more than a political framework to survive and to serve Africa. The answer must be in the religion-cultural framework, within which all disciplines must be located: political, sociological, economic, environmental and religious. What is needed is a spiritual base to guide and inform the life of Africa."

The intention of inter-faith dialogue in Africa must be to work towards an authentic African community ... In this process our religions will move from being competitors building religious edifices, to being channels of a spirituality that is life-giving, community building, socially relevant, offering real hope not pious promises.

★ ★ ★ ★

Not everyone will agree with Cedric especially if you're not a socialist or if you believe that your religion or denomination is the only true one. Whatever your thoughts on those issues are, don't lose sight of what he is saying about faith and political activity especially when he says, "Oppressed, tortured, imprisoned, with no hope or vision except our own, we had a vivid living powerful experience of faith that liberation was on the way and power was in the people," (and he should know). "Amandla," he says, "Out of the crucible emerged refreshing prophetic experiences ...."

For me, Cedric is one of those modern day prophets with a vision for South Africa that needs to be exported to Europe if it is ever going to have a soul.

Not long after the Asian Tsunami disaster he sent the following text, which fits perfectly with what he had written above.

The earthquake which ripped a thousand kilometer slice in the floor of the Indian Ocean on 26th December 2004 also revealed fault lines in popular ideas about God. Now the physical and emotional shocks have subsided, people are assessing the spiritual tremors.

Since the Scientific Revolution began in the 16th century, many sincere religious people have questioned traditional teaching about God. The early myths of a loving Father up in the sky, blessing or punishing, don't add up anymore.

The hypotheses of heaven and hell ring fewer bells. Many congregants wriggle with embarrassment over inherited beliefs, but lack the expertise or courage to question them. Theology is an unfolding revelation, a book of many chapters probing a meaningful framework for human life and a new chapter is being written now.

Attention has moved from science **versus** faith to science **and** faith, from a self-centered obsession with our own souls to the role of human community. Today's cosmic theology embraces everything from deep space to the pulse beat of Earthly humanity. Homo sapiens is part of the evolution of Earth. We are not outsiders, but insiders who emerged on this ball of rock and water in a breath of air only three miles thick, where things go bump in the night like volcanoes, epidemics, droughts and tsunamis. Earth operates within the dictates of its own structures from the Big Bang to particle physics, and we are part of these 'forces of nature'. It has been an incredible process. Professor Brian Swimme writes:

"The image I like is this: you have molten rock, and then all by itself, it transforms into a human mother caring for her child. That's a rather astounding transformation. Of course, it takes four billion years. You've got silica, you've got magnesium. You've got all the elements of rock, and it becomes the translucent blue eyes, and beautiful brown hair and this deep sense of love and concern and even sacrifice for the child. That is a deep transfiguration. Love and truth and compassion and zest and all these qualities that we regard as divine become more powerfully embodied in the universe."

Human nature has three elements: body, mind, and spirit working in community, which demands that we relate to others with care, compassion, sharing, generosity and honesty. It is spirit which directs what minds think *and bodies do. Spiritual power is the secular guts of political, economic and cultural processes in the community.*

*So success is not in coddling our souls to curry favour with God in heaven, but in building humanity for the good of all. Community emerges by engaging the challenges of nature, politics, an economy that benefits all humanity, and the spiritual awareness that stops religions from demonising one another. Life is driven by the spirit in **us**, the ground of **our** being, not something in space. Madiba said recently: "My wish is that South Africans never give up their belief in goodness, that they may cherish that faith in human beings as a cornerstone of our democracy."*

Tsunami is a typical Earth event. Lightning strikes. Many fell off whilst domesticating animals, went hungry learning to cultivate vegetables, and died in Comet airliners whilst discovering metal fatigue.

Catastrophes far worse than a tsunami, occur about every 500 million years and at least five have almost extinguished life on Earth. The last of these, about 250 million years ago, seemingly saw an asteroid blast a hundred kilometer crater near Mexico which shook and warmed the globe, poisoned the atmosphere, and wiped out the dinosaurs. It also cleared the stage for the mammals, including the humans. Enter us.

Asking 'Why does God allow it?' is the wrong question, like 'Why is ice-cream cold?' It is part of being human. It is through collective conquests from microbes to meteors that this incredible human-ness has emerged. But now we are facing a sixth extinction.

Tsunami disasters will still happen—the San Andreas fault in California can blow at any moment—but the major peril today is that humanity has lost the plot. We are causing global warming, environmental destruction, war and overpopulation which will extinguish centuries of life in a dozen disastrous decades unless we change it.

Humanity is cursed by evil forces pretending they are good. We have allowed our creative zest to be hijacked by self-centred, competitive, political, economic and religious structures which think they are gods. Sweeping over us like a tsunami wave, individualism, capitalism, and fundamentalism have brought humanity to the brink of oblivion. The answer is to unite and regenerate the spiritual dynamics of our nature.

We can rediscover human community, not as individuals opting out and going to heaven, but as the end-product of millions of years of evolution upon Earth. It is a reorientation of belief like being born again, a creative leap which has prompted ecumenical inter-faith movements, the United Nations, a globalised economy, instant communication, and a spate of quests for new spiritual initiatives in this post-religious age.

This is where God-thought helps. We must not permit some religious institutions with pre-scientific views of Creation to destroy the spiritual teaching of the great prophets. God is in the tsunami because God is embedded in the actual process of the Universe, Earth and Humanity. God is the spiritual reality in us, the deep destiny who shapes our future. Human creation is a caring compassionate community within which God copes with physical and spiritual tsunamis. God suffers too because God is love. That's the way it is.

This happy-creative leap of belief enables us, for example, to reclaim the Good News of Jesus about the Ruling Power of God in the inter-faith, here-and-now, human collective. God's liberating power comes through love in the human community: that is the gospel. Love is the secular-spiritual dynamic which can overcome the tsunami of political violence, economic poverty-making, and religious misconceptions. Devout paleontologist Teilhard de Chardin wrote:

"The day will come when we shall harness for God the energies of love. And on that day, for the second time in the history of the world, the human being will have discovered fire."

Faith does not see the future in sky god dogmas, but in the faith energy of caring. The strategic perspective of secular spirituality reaches out like the finger of God to Adam on the Sistine Chapel ceiling—pointing even to other worlds and other millions of years.

This secular spirituality has its feet on the ground in Africa. Africa's holistic approach to life is not packaged in religious institutional boxes. Despite arguments over details, we know the Luthuli-Tambo-Mandela-Mbeki years have set us on a different way of life. The Liberation Struggle, African Renaissance and African Union arise from the conviction that humanity can find the answers.

The western Oppressive Empire seeks like a black hole to suck us all into its *destructive, political, economic and religious structures, but our vision is to liberate and transform society. Apartheid was only a practice session. In questing a progressive, healed Africa together we experience the spiritual dynamic of being fully human.*

This is the positive input of a Tsunami theology. Humanity perches on a living Earth and is part of its evolution. Through these physical and mental challenges rises our faith in the spiritual power of God-in-us. We can turn our backs on the false gods because they will never arrive on a heavenly helicopter to lift us out of the storm; we can face the demons together; we can re-experience the creative potential God has put in the human initiative. It is a humbling and empowering opportunity.

The tsunami of individualism, capitalism and fundamentalism threatens us with the sixth extinction. Our task is to inspire and mobilise the progressive forces to liberate ourselves. The Good News is that we can.

★ ★ ★ ★

People like Cedric, or Desmond Tutu, or Boris Trajkovski or countless others have their beliefs intertwined with their politics. They are inseparable.

As I write this I am "a senior politician" in the European Parliament and seen as a 'doyen d'age'. Most of my generation had plenty of life experiences before getting elected to any kind of position. My 12 years in the Merchant Navy, my time in industry, in chemical plants and shipyards has given me plenty of the real world to bring into politics. I came into politics as most of my contemporaries did, as a vocation, in my case driven by my beliefs. It was done in an attempt to do the things that Cedric writes about, simply to make the world a better place, to attempt to get human beings to live peacefully and co-operatively with one another. Politics is a vocation or it is nothing. Okay there must have been something about self-aggrandizement but I fail to see it staring me in the face when someone becomes a local Councillor and their careers and pensions are put in jeopardy and their family lives take second place.

My worry today is that too many people (and dare I say it, young people) come into politics for a job. That sounds like a grumpy old man and many of my very good, young colleagues will not thank me for saying that. Actually one of the Dutch MEPs, Michael van Hulton, left the Parliament after five years because he wanted experience in the real world. He had come straight from being academically educated into politics and he realized that he was missing those life experiences outside of politics.

I could add that of the 19 British Labour MEPs, I am now the only one to have had a career in industry, as opposed to teaching or the law, or being in the public service sector. Although being a professional actor, as my colleague Michael Cashman was, is very hard work. What I am trying to say is that politics needs people of many backgrounds to reflect the people we represent. It's at this point I'm in danger of repeating gripes from my previous book so I'll stop.

But whatever background you are from you still have to be motivated by a belief in ideals not simply because it's a career.

What I would really like is for the experiences of the people mentioned in this book, like Cedric, to have an effect on those who feel they can contribute to politics. That means being a prophet and putting a soul into politics

SIX

I get delivered on a weekly basis *The Methodist Recorder*, the newspaper of the Methodist Church in the UK. I seldom read all of it, in fact there are times when I seldom read it at all. A quick glance through, picking out the pieces that would really interest me and trying to read them on a plane or travelling somewhere is probably closer to reality.

One week in January 2000, as I browsed through it, I landed on the book review page, which I never read. Let me stress I never (never say never, you're a politician, Terry), okay, I seldom ever read the book review page. This time I stopped and read a review of a book by some American politician, I can't remember what it actually said but I distinctly remembered the title *Lessons from a Father to his Son*. End of story, or so I thought.

Paul Petrie had fixed up the invitation to attend the National Prayer Breakfast in Washington at the start of February that year. As part of the three-day event, the organisers try to arrange meetings between American politicians and visiting politicians for informal discussions. I had a few meetings fixed up and Paul recommended that I should go with a Dutch MEP colleague, Rijk van Damme, to see this particular Senator. Rijk was elected on a right wing, fundamental Christian ticket in The Netherlands and whilst our politics were poles apart he was a nice guy and I didn't mind going with him.

So we went and were introduced to John Ashcroft, the Republican Senator for Missouri. As we began to talk he told us how he had been the Governor of Missouri from 1984 to 1992 and had been in the Senate since 1994. He liked to sing, had a good voice and had formed a group of elected representatives to perform. He was good company and helped us relax. As he unfolded his story he mentioned his book, to which I said, "I've just read a review of it, it's called 'Lessons from a father to his son.'" You can imagine his surprise and delight as I began to remember what I had read. Here he was this right wing

Republican, a devout Christian, one who had no qualms about expressing his faith publicly, who asked us to pray with him before we left and we did, and I was trying to figure him out.

Figure him out as a Christian when politically, like Rijk, we were poles apart. I remembered the bit in the book about capital punishment so I raised it and we discussed it.

I asked how he could as a Christian support capital punishment, how he could not pardon someone when he had the power to do so. What follows is an extract from the book but it is almost word for word how it was relayed to us that day:

> As history would have it, the practice of executing murderers, which had long been frozen by our judicial system, began to thaw during my first term as Missouri's Chief Executive. Suddenly the governor's office operated as the final appeal for men on death row and this created serious pressure on me personally.
>
> Among those sentenced to death was one who had managed to get married during his time on death row. His wife would come to church occasionally, sitting close to me. Once she spoke very briefly to me, but most often I think she just wanted me to sense her presence, perhaps hoping I would somehow respond by pardoning the killer.
>
> And then there were the letters.
>
> You can feel the pressure of a letter written: "Dear Governor, You now hold a man's life in your hands. He has been sentenced to die, but you need to know that he has become a Christian. He is truly repentant and sorry for what he has done, so I'm asking you to commute his death sentence to life in prison. After all, he's not just a criminal—at least, not anymore. He is now a brother in the Lord."
>
> Answering that kind of mail is not easy.
>
> Because our lives have meaning, there are consequences to our actions, and we must learn to accept them. Our culture is infected with the thought that freedom means the lack of consequences, but the laws of nature and of nature's God know that there are no inconsequential acts—which bring us

back to my decision about the man who was sentenced to death.

On the day that any execution was scheduled, I lived with a constant awareness of what was about to take place. I had received the appeals long in advance and had organised teams of attorneys who would send me thick files full of documentation. The attorneys had carefully reviewed the information. I told them to bring to my attention any salient points or any compelling reasons why the judgement of the people of the state should not be carried out.

Even when everything appeared to be in order, I would stay in my office or near a handy telephone in case there was an extraordinary or late-breaking development. This was not likely. Most of the men sentenced to die had been convicted eight to twelve years prior, and their cases had travelled through numerous legal reviews and evaluations at virtually every level of the judicial system.

I had to learn not to assume responsibility that was not mine. My decision was whether to interrupt the process, not whether I would kill. Though that decision is a weighty one, it would be equally sobering to say to the people of Missouri that their system has not worked.

I chose not to commute this man's death sentence. Just because a murderer has learned to love the Lord does not mean the state should pardon him. As a Christian, I am willing to forgive him; but as a governor, it would have been inappropriate for me to pardon him unless a mistake had been made in the judicial proceedings.

My guiding philosophy was fairly simple: state law had given me powers as governor for a particular purpose. If the people had somehow convicted someone who did not warrant conviction, I was to step in and correct it. It was not my responsibility to second-guess the people; it would have been arrogant and irresponsible for me to commute every death sentence, or the death sentences passed on newly converted Christians, arguing, "The law says this is to happen, but I'm going to replace that law with my own opinion."

It was the ultimate appeal to correct error, not reward regrets, emotion, or even religious conversion. Becoming a Christian may remove us from eternal penalties, but it does not relieve us or others from the consequences of our acts.

73

In the end, capital punishment saves lives. Even though I believe this, following through was never an easy task.

He also explained to us, and it's also in the book, that Ronald Reagan when President of the USA had once spoken to a group of Attorney Generals, of which John Ashcroft was chairman, about the dilemma he had faced when he had been Governor of California on this issue, Reagan said that after a highly publicised execution he received a message in his mail that said, "Governor, thanks for saving my life. I'm seventy years old and my wife and I run a liquor store. Last week a thug broke in while we were there. He intended to rob us, but I resisted him. He wrestled me to the floor, and once I was pinned down, he poised his knife above my throat. I had both my hands on his wrists, struggling with all my might to stop him from killing me. As I grew weaker and weaker, I finally shouted out, 'Go ahead and kill me! You'll get the death penalty and be executed, just like the guy last week.' He dropped his knife and ran from the store. Thank you, Governor. Your fortitude and resolve saved my life."

John Ashcroft, who at the time of writing is the Attorney General in the Bush Administration, says that Reagan supported capital punishment because of this story and no doubt he also uses it. But as a Christian who is against capital punishment, I had to try to understand his way of thinking. Is this a difference of politics, left versus right, or is there a Christian dimension to this?

Is his argument that it was his duty as governor to simply ensure that the law of the State was carried out a valid one? Did he ever try to change the law of the State? He makes it clear that he supports capital punishment, yet would he have acted in the same manner if he had not supported the death penalty for instance. Would he have reacted to those pleas of commuting the sentence to life imprisonment? Only he can answer these questions and, unfortunately, I never asked him.

As I write this, I am reminded of the comments of a colleague and friend Ari Vattenen, a Finn, former world champion rally driver, an MEP for Finland from 1999 to 2004 and then elected in France as an MEP in 2004. During our discussions at our monthly prayer breakfast Ari often makes his views known on being against capital punishment. He is also pro-life and is very anti-abortion (from deep felt personal experience) and argues that life is sacred, so how can someone like John Ashcroft be pro-life and support killing convicted people? That's the question that should have been asked of Senator Ashcroft and I'm sure Ari would have asked him had he been there.

During that same visit to Washington, and at one of the meetings between politicians from overseas and the Congress, I met Tony Hall, a Congressman from Dayton, Ohio, a politician who changed his mind about capital punishment and abortion. He is also a voice for the world's poor and oppressed.

Members of Congress are elected every two years, which means they spend all their time electioneering for the next vote. As one Democrat Congressman said to me, "Every Thursday my job is to go to Democrat headquarters, get on the telephone and spend all day fundraising to pay for the next election." I suppose this is one of the reasons why few American politicians have a grasp of international affairs.

One Congressman, however, was different in that he had a knowledge of, and had visited, some of the world's trouble spots, including Sudan and North Korea. He had also fought his last election without spending a penny. This was not your normal American Lower House representative.

I met him in Washington, then in Brussels when he was the guest speaker at the annual European Prayer Breakfast. By this time, he had been appointed the U.S. Ambassador to the World Food Programme based in Rome. I also had the chance to meet him in this role in Brussels and in Rome. The interview I did with him was quite fascinating.

When Tony Hall was elected to Congress 24 years previously, he wasn't a Christian, and didn't know much about God. He described himself as having "great respect for Him, but…He wasn't in my environment or in my arena." Even though he was a successful sports and business man, and was then elected to Congress, which "as a politician in America, it is one of the great places to be," he felt something was missing. "You know, if this is it in life we're getting cheated. If being successful, being ambitious and achieving, if that's what life is all about, something is wrong here." He went to a prayer breakfast led by Chuck Colson of Watergate fame, and "had never heard anybody ever talk like him." He was "overwhelmed by the way he spoke." His original reasoning for attending such an event was, "I need some of this God stuff to rub off on me…it'll look good and people will think 'what a good man this is'." Tony didn't remember everything Chuck said, just that it was about God, and it really touched him. "Chuck had been in jail, and I was stunned that he would be so sincere and so humble and so real about faith." Chuck's testimony inspired him to "hunt" for God, and he began attending different churches after being elected to Congress. His wife would ask, "What's wrong with you?"

Tony tells of how he was "embarrassed to ask anybody, because I didn't know anybody that knew anything about God and I was embarrassed to say 'I need help and I'm looking for God', but I didn't know where to look." He was then "befriended" by a freshman Congressman and was invited to dinner where he heard a guest called Bill Bright speak. "As soon as this guy started talking about Jesus I knew that that was it, that was what I was looking for." At dinner Tony saw Bill, and the people that were around him and thought "Whatever they got I want." His describes how when he went home that night he "accepted it" and "wanted it." "For a year I was bubbly, excited, I was nuts about God, and everybody I knew I would tell." None of his friends were Christians, and he hadn't wanted to be around Christians, thinking he wouldn't have any fun. Tony explains that "People would come over to my house and they'd say: 'What's new?' and I'd say: 'You're not going to believe this, but I believe in Jesus.' Eyeballs would click to the ceiling, my wife would sigh and kick me under the table. She'd say 'What, are you nuts? You're not going to have any friends! Quit doing that.' I said: 'I know'. Then every night I would ask her for six months: 'Would you pray that prayer with me to receive Jesus?' And she would get even more mad, saying, 'You have no right to do that!'"

Eventually Tony stopped asking his wife to become a Christian. "I learnt my first lesson with the Lord—you can't push Him down people's throats 'cause people will run. I was trying to push Him down my wife's throat and she was running from Him. I looked like a nut case to her. Six months later she became a believer. I said: 'Why?' She said: 'When you stopped preaching, then I saw your life change, and your life really changed in front of my eyes. Maybe you didn't see it, but I saw it.' And at that time we had picked a church that I really felt very good about, and that started my walk." Once settled in a church, some of Tony's politics changed. "As I began to read the Bible, I began to see on certain issues, for example, glaring issues like abortion, that I was wrong, I was voting for abortion when I first went there because I didn't know any better, I didn't have a foundation. I didn't know that it was wrong, but I felt that it was wrong to vote this way. And when I was reading the scripture one night I thought; 'It must have been the Holy Spirit speaking through the Word. I thought; 'I'm wrong....I have been wrong.' Of course, a

Democrat voting pro-life, that was very different in those days and so I received a lot of grief, but I changed the next day and never changed back since then. So that was one thing that really changed, and the other thing that changed, it gave me focus—more focus than I've ever had, and enabled me to focus in on things that are very important to me like human rights, hunger and poverty."

Tony had much opposition to his stance on abortion. "A lot of my liberal friends wouldn't give me any money and a lot of people, especially Democrats, you'd mention my name and they'd spit, 'cause they couldn't believe that a guy in the Democratic party would believe this way. Other times I had voted with the Conservative part of the Congress very difficult budget issues. Sometimes you have to go against your constituency. You don't like it but you have to go against them because you know more about the issue, it's more of a principle than anything. I went to a town hall meeting. I walked in, everybody in the place got up and booed me." He thought he would be voted out of office. "I was voting on something of conscience and my district perceived it as being nuts, very wrong. I had prayed about this vote, one of the first times as a believer I had prayed which way to go. Not that the Lord came down and said vote this way or that way, but I was learning and going against what would be a common practice for a Democrat. My staff thought my career was over on that vote, but actually the next time I ran nobody ran against me."

The religious right dominate certain issues in the United States. Tony explained, "Certain issues I might even agree with, like abortion, or maybe positions on homosexuality, but they do it in such a harsh way that it's accusatory, it's judgmental, it's not loving. When you judge somebody without love, I think that defeats and hurts the cause of Jesus." Apparently some people say: 'Tony Hall is not a Christian because out of 10 votes he only voted seven times, or no, he only voted twice or three times out of ten votes with us'." Tony told me, "I've always voted for the death penalty but in recent years I've changed, because of the Huderite religious community. They're really good and decent people, but the kids came in one time and challenged me on my position on capital punishment so I went back and searched the Scriptures. If you look at the Scriptures you can see both sides. I voted for capital punishment for many years, but in the last couple of years of being a Congressman I decided that I was wrong, I just felt that I was going the wrong way, that the government doesn't have the right to take innocent life. It doesn't mean that people don't deserve punishment, but I felt to go as far as we have done, to take a life like that in our system was wrong. Plus it was unfair, because there weren't any women or rich people getting executed. It was all poor people, and most were blacks, and so it was very discriminatory. It was never fair or equal."

"I think Jesus said this, he said: 'I didn't give you the arm for nothing. I didn't give you the power for nothing', which you could interpret as to mean: 'I gave you the power, you can use it via the government.' Do we have the right to take life? You know, I always used to interpret that and say 'yes'. But, I think we do have the right to defend ourselves, we have the right to go to war, we are the arm. But because our law on capital punishment has been so discriminating and not fair, I mean, a poor person, they don't have a chance in our system. Whether they're guilty or not guilty, I mean, their chances are not good. So to me it's not a very fair law. So with that in mind I began to change and these kids worked on me. I didn't know them and they'd never voted for me and it didn't matter what they felt about me, but I began to think more and more about the issue and thinking that I might be wrong about this issue."

Apart from his politics, he explained faith has given him more focus than ever before, enabling him to fully address issues such as human rights, hunger and poverty. After a year of being a Christian, a friend asked him, "Don't you think its time to start bringing Jesus into your workplace?" Tony knew he was making a valid point, but didn't know how to do it. He didn't want to look like "a crazy man, or a nut case," just bring Jesus' values into his work "in a way that's honouring" and not drawing publicity to himself; "I don't think God wants me to do that but I knew that he was right and I began to pray about it." In 1984 he went to Ethiopia and was shocked by the situation, by "seeing death up close…it was a horrendous week." When he returned home he thought, "This is what he was talking about. There are over 2,500 verses in the Bible that deal with orphans and widows and the sick and people in prison." He realised that outside of taking care of his district, this would then be his focus.

I asked Tony what he thought about the moral rights and wrongs of American politics when huge amounts of money are spent on electioneering. He believes that this is not right, and told me "I never had to do it, and that was I think a gift of God." I also questioned him on how he managed to support overseas projects. He told me, "I began to get letters and phone calls saying: 'Look, you care more about people in Ethiopia than you do in main street, and I thought; 'Uh oh, I'm in trouble here. If I don't find a way of bringing this issue home I'm in trouble.' There were folk on the poverty line in Ohio. So we did a fast for 40 hours and for every hour we'd fast, we'd get people or businesses to back us. So over one weekend we raised something like $380,000. If you wanted it to go to 'World Vision', to Ethiopia, if you wanted it to go to the Jewish Release Group, it went there. We'd send it wherever you wanted it and then half of it stayed in Dayton. 3,000 people fasted with me that week. That built a constituency, then we started a senior citizen feeding programme and then we had about 600 volunteers that would do that every Saturday. Then we started an immunisation programme, then we started a gleaning programme. If you don't take care of home, you won't get elected and they won't let you take care of the Third World. If you tell them and educate them on what you're doing, they always make the right decision."

Tony explained that when he became a Christian, life, "in many ways it got tougher. I had more peace, but there has been a lot of turmoil in my life and I lost a son to cancer. He was sick for three years and we struggled with him and struggled with him; and he was such a sweet boy, nice boy, a good kid. To go through that day in and day out, it was really, really hard. It just brought us up and down...he's going to live, he's not going to live, he's going to live. He had so many ups and downs it was unbelievable and there were days there where we felt we were just hanging on the cliff by our finger nails. It was hard to get through the day. He died, and it devastated us, but a very interesting thing happened to me, as sick and frustrated as I was, my faith got stronger, and I can't tell you why. Sometimes I was really, really mad at God; I would take it out on Him. When things were going bad with my son and he'd be bleeding and just...to see a son be tortured like that, and you'd just want to jump off the building or you'd want to scream or run your head through the wall or something. There was a time that I raged against Him and, you know, if you go through this for three years, I mean, it just never stopped, never stopped. And there was one night when I challenged Him to come down for a fight, and I was so mad. It was such a terrible day for my son. He was hurting so bad. My wife and I were hurting, we were just dying inside, and I asked Him to come down because I wanted to punch Him out. Then I said: 'Then you can kill me, but I want to take one shot at you.' Of course he never did, I never got my shot and I'm very glad I didn't. I did pray though. I kept praying: 'Lord, whatever happens I know that you are Lord. I don't want to lose my faith, so don't let me lose my faith.' I came through it stronger." When I asked him if he ever asked God why, he told me, "All the time. I don't think there is an answer, I don't think we're going to know until we meet the Lord. At one point in his ministry, Jesus began to say things like: 'I am the bread of life' and 'Drink my blood'. He lost a lot of believers. He said to Peter: 'Are you going to leave?' Peter said to Him: 'Where am I going? You are the Lord, my God. I'm staying with you.' That's the way I felt. I didn't have any place to go. I know that He's God. I know that He's Lord. I know that He's good. I don't understand things that He does, but I trust Him." I asked him has he ever given that testimony in public. He said that he'd never given the details of it. "I occasionally have said in some of my speaking sometimes about.....you know, a lot of people believe that believers lead a model life and they don't have any turmoil. That's not true. As a matter of fact, one thing you can be assured of, you are going to have ups and downs. You're going to have them. So occasionally I have talked about it, but never in detail like that."

Tony Hall's attitude and that of Paul Petrie (see Chapter 8) are so much alike, when they can have so much heartache and yet still commune with God. Paul explains it by saying it's only possible when you have a personal relationship with God. It's not just a matter of professing to be a Christian, it really is a matter of 'knowing' God, of being in a prayerful dialogue with Him. Too many people, when they do pray, are invariably asking for something, whereas meaningful prayer is about praise, confession, thanks, sharing anxieties or worries, and intercession, and doing it in the presence of God and feeling that presence. It's that relationship that could make Tony Hall rant and rave at God. You can't do it if you don't know Him. I've done it myself. My daughter-in-law Gill, when she was pregnant for the second time, went for her 12 week scan. Doris and I were in Heathrow airport waiting to fly out to Athens when her mobile phone rang. It was our son David, distraught with the news that the baby had been dead for about 10 days. It was a gut-wrenching feeling, but when all the tears had been shed and with the passing of time and the realisation that one in four pregnancies didn't make it, then we could accept that perhaps it was just one of those things. Yes, I had prayed for Gill and the baby, but......Gill became pregnant again and all the family were thrilled. This time my prayers were more than meaningful, they were a real plea that everything would be fine this time. I'd arrived in Brussels early one evening, and went to the Parliament; there were few people about. As I walked down a deserted corridor my mobile telephone rang and it was Doris to tell me that exactly the same thing had occurred again, the baby was dead. I reached my office, my mind in turmoil, trying to figure out what was going on. So much prayer had been invested in this. What was the point of it, what was your game, God? Then I exploded and raged against God. I'd never called Him a bastard before. I had the Barbara Dührkop feeling of not liking Him. It wasn't fair, it just wasn't fair. My relationship with God became strained and more formal, but as Paul Petrie would explain to me some time later when I spoke to him about it, I can only feel that way if I had that relationship with Him. Like Tony Hall, whatever He was putting us through, he was still God and there was no other to rage at or talk to.

Anne Hall, our Minister from my local Methodist Church, came to see me to ask how I was and I explained that I was working my way through it. She had had enough problems in her own life to know how I felt and she helped. Anne always says that when you love someone then you are going to get hurt because you feel for them, you feel their hurt and pain and suffering, and all that comes with love.

When Gill became pregnant for a third time, she had a scan at six weeks and a heart beat was detected, but once again at 12 weeks the baby was dead. "It's just bad luck," said the doctor. There was nothing wrong that they could see. When David telephoned home to tell us, this time he wasn't in tears. Maybe it was a matter of "It's what we've come to expect." My heart sank, I felt tremendous sadness, especially for David and Gill, but there was no rage this time. I'd learnt not to ask why.

Shortly after, I was preaching in our church on Mothers' Day. My theme was the Prodigal Son and how, for many years, I could never understand the actions of the father. My sympathies were always with the son who had stayed behind. Here was a waster who had blown his inheritance, then came home when things got rough. It was only when I became a father myself and realised that you can love your children just as much when they are 18 years old as you could when they are 18 days or 18 months old. Even now with David and Joanne, my daughter, both in their thirties, I still have that same love. The point I was making in the sermon is that this is the love that God our father has for us. No matter how we treat Him, He is still prepared to accept us for all our faults. And if that's how a father could feel then how would a mother more so react. I finished the sermon by quoting Philip Yancey, this time from 'Where is God When it Hurts?'

'For a good portion of my life, I shared the perspective of those who rail against God for allowing pain. Suffering pressed in too close. I could find no way to rationalise a world as toxic as this one. As I visited people whose pain far exceeded my own, though, I was surprised by its effects. Suffering seemed as likely to reinforce faith as to sow agnosticism. The problem of pain will have no solution until God recreates the earth. I am sustained by faith in that great hope. If I did not truly believe that God is a physician and not a sadist, I would abandon all attempt to plumb the mystery of suffering. My anger about pain has melted for one reason: I have come to know God. He has given me joy and love and happiness and goodness. They have come in unexpected flashes, in the midst of my confused, imperfect world, but they have been enough to convince me that my God is worthy of trust. Knowing Him is worth all enduring.'

As I spoke I began to choke up and I could feel the emotion in my voice and tears in my eyes as I said the words: "He has given me joy and love and happiness and goodness." Because he has and I know how blessed I have been in my life to have the family I have and the opportunities granted me throughout my life.

I continually thank God for what I have had in this life and that relationship with him is priceless.

SEVEN

Many people view the Rev. Ian Paisley, MP, former MEP, MLA (Member of the Legislative Assembly for Northern Ireland), and leader of the Democratic Unionist Party, DUP, as the scourge of Roman Catholics and 'Popery' as he would call it. He seems to have been around forever, causing trouble about the Roman Catholic Church, attacking Republicanism and defending Ulster's right to remain British.

Every time you saw him on television, whether in a studio or on the news, he wore the same scowling countenance and had the same powerful voice bellowing out in his familiar Ulster accent. "No Surrender" was his rallying cry as he typified the popular English perception of the Protestant Ulsterman.

He had been an elected MEP since 1979 and served in the European Parliament for 25 years. I bumped into him infrequently and when Brian Simpson and I formed the all-party Rugby League Intergroup of MEPs, his son, Ian Paisley Junior, came along to find out what it was about. We would chat on the odd occasions that he and I were in the Parliament together. What became obvious was that this man, who was portrayed as the Devil incarnate was actually a good constituency Member, working for his constituents of whatever religion. He also had a good sense of humour, which had never ever come across on the television screen. I remember once when the Archbishop of Canterbury was addressing a meeting in the Parliament and Ian said something like: "I know you call us fundamentalists, funny mentalists...." In normal conversation with him, forgetting the persona that was portrayed by the media, he was quite a likeable character. He never came to our monthly prayer breakfast in Strasbourg and he never came to the annual European Prayer Breakfast. I realised that I had never discussed religion with him, never mind religion and politics. So not long before his retirement from the European Parliament, I asked him if I could record an interview with him, to which he willingly consented. By this time he was ageing and the 'Big Man' was not as tall in stature as he had been, nor was his voice at the decibel level of times past. I wanted to know how someone like him said and did the things he did in the name of God in a political arena. This was no Ulrich Meisel, or Maat Laar, or Tony Hall; it wasn't even John Ashcroft. This was the unique Ian Paisley and what follows is an abridged version of the interview.

TERRY WYNN: But how do you describe your Christianity?

IAN PAISLEY: Well I would be what to you as a Methodist knowing your history, I would be a 'Bible Christian', the Bible is the religion of Protestants, then I would be a Bible Christian, and when I say that, I believe the Bible is the Word of God; I believe that it is firmly inspired, I believe that it has this whole role of faith in practice and I would take my stand on what the Bible says, and accept it with humility, but with faith.

TERRY WYNN: But I don't have a problem with that; I have a lot of friends who would be in exactly the same position, but your fame, or infamy came from your condemnation of, I've got to be careful how I say this, was it just popery, or the Roman Catholic Church, or Catholics?

IAN PAISLEY: Well not Catholics, many Catholics vote for me. It's not Catholics; it's the system. I'm not against the people, I'm against the system, just the same way as I love sinners, but I don't love their sins, and I take that example from the Lord Jesus, who was a lover of sinners but not a lover of their sins, and because a man condemns the sins of people doesn't mean he's condemning them; in fact he's trying to save them because its just like a man in a house fire, I mean I condemn the person that settled into the house, but I'm going to get them right out of the fire...the brand plucked from the burning.

TERRY WYNN: So where did the anti-popery come from? For the uninitiated, why did you play such a part?

IAN PAISLEY: Well...because that is the real crux of the battle between a pre-Reformation Roman dogma and a return to Bible teaching, and that is where the parting of the ways is, it was the parting of the ways of the Reformation, and it will always be the parting of the ways...I don't see any relationship whatsoever between a system that elevates a man, that puts him in as the Vicar of Christ, declares that what he says from the chair of St Peter is ex-cathedra and must be accepted, and the infallible book. I accept the word of the God and not the word of the pope. And, er, this, of course, runs deep in my country, because my country was first of all planted by Scots Presbyterians of the theology of John Knox; they suffered for their faith; they were martyred, we had the terrible parallel martyring like they had in France: the St Bartholomew's massacre was in 1643 innovated in our country when our rivers ran red with the blood of Protestants. So we have suffered for our faith, and therefore our faith is a real thing. But, that is not to say that we do not love our own fellow Roman Catholic countrymen, because I believe the very ethic of the Bible is that you love your neighbour as yourself. And who is your neighbour? Your neighbour is the person that needs your need, a needy person, I mean that's how the Lord defined it, and I believe that that is what we've got to do, that's why I'm delighted when I have people coming to my surgeries, which are always strong with people with complaints, and I ask them, 'Well who sent you?' They said the local priest sent us, they said the big man will look after you well, he's a neighbour.

TERRY WYNN: You always had a reputation for being a good constituency MP anyway.

IAN PAISLEY: That's right. I don't think you can separate your religion from your politics, its just like this here: If I am a grocer, and I'm a Christian, then I'll be a Christian grocer, if I'm a politician and a Christian then I'll be a Christian politician.

TERRY WYNN: How do you the explain to the Roman Catholics who come to your surgeries your disdain for the position of the Pope?

IAN PAISLEY: Well, they all accept it, they accept it quite naturally, I mean the Roman Catholic church disdains us, they don't believe that any Protestant minister is a minister at all, not even recognised. Take the Roman Catholic church's attitude. I mean there's nobody any good except you abide by what they say, I mean even recently they wouldn't even give communion to people...

TERRY WYNN: So where did the politics start, and why?

IAN PAISLEY: Well, the politics didn't start because brought up in the atmosphere of er the faith the protestant faith in Northern Ireland, its part of the political thing, nationalism is to a great extent...

TERRY WYNN: Are you an Orangeman?

IAN PAISLEY: Not now, I was an Orangeman, but I separated from the Orange order because of ecumenism, I felt that they were leaving their basic standards, therefore I no longer belong to them.

But I'm very friendly with them; they use our building for their services. There are two, of course, orders in Ireland, there's the Independent Orange Order and the Official order and they are both getting more and more friendly thanks to my good graces with both of them. But I mean I have distinctive views from both of them. I have distinctive views and I have to be distinctive in those views otherwise people say he's a hypocrite; if you're going to take a stand you have to take it everywhere; that's what I think. But I don't have any difficulty with the Roman Catholic population because they know me, who I am; they've been greatly helped by me in many ways...

TERRY WYNN: But you just said the politics didn't start. Being part of the scene in Ulster, before I interrupted you, you were going to say being part of the scene in Ulster where politics is endemic..

IAN PAISLEY: That's right, and I believe it should be endemic.

TERRY WYNN: Were you ever in the Ulster Unionist party?

IAN PAISLEY: I was, I was.

TERRY WYNN: And at what age?

IAN PAISLEY: Oh, an early age, 18, 19; I was one of their agents, won them seats and various councils in the old Stormont, in their higher councils.

TERRY WYNN: So when did you decide to stand for office yourself?

IAN PAISLEY: Well this came about actually through the services of the Prime Minister a man called O'Neil, Terence O'Neil, who was not a traditional unionist but played the orange card and played traditional unionism for election purposes, but then when he got into office he went against everything that was traditionally unionist and there was a big rumpus in the party just as there is over Mr Trimble today... (laughs) And some of us felt that the time had come when we would have to show that there was a strong segment of unionism that didn't approve of this and the only way you can really show that as the Labour party actually learnt in history, is by putting up candidates, there's no use telling people that you're for them if you never run a candidate, so we had to run, so we started running candidates, and these candidates did exceptionally well, because we touched a spot; we also touched a spot as far as working for the people, you can't, you can never divide, you can't say that it was a particular doctrine that we held, it was the doctrine of the practice, because we are practising politicians. If a man is troubled and he has something wrong about his education, and the education of his children, about his house, about his roads. I mean we are the servants, I mean our slogan is surrender never, but service ever.

TERRY WYNN: David Trimble I presume would say that he was a Christian, would he?

IAN PAISLEY: Oh he would, he would.

TERRY WYNN: Well I'm sure he is, he is.

IAN PAISLEY: Well, he would be a professing Christian in the sense that he professes to it being a profession. He's an Orangeman, of course, as well.

TERRY WYNN: So what would be the difference between David Trimble as a Christian in politics in Ulster and you?

IAN PAISLEY: Well I er, well my Christianity would make me tell the truth no matter how humiliating it might be, I mean I'm never afraid to tell the truth, I mean, that's what I say to people "Look, I am a democrat. I come out and tell the worst things about myself; I tell, you, I don't put it in nice sugar coated words, I speak what I say." I mean even John Major, of all people, said to me "Ian, you're the only politician, of note, that writes to me that I don't need clarification." But I think that's a very good testimony. I'm sorry I didn't get him to sign it! But then his own reputation's not too good for honesty! (laughing) So it perhaps wouldn't have done me any good.

TERRY WYNN: Do you consider Roman Catholic Christians to have a faith as strong as you?

IAN PAISLEY: I believe that Christianity has nothing to do with denominations. I believe that there are Roman Catholic Christians, because the Bible makes it clear that there are within the church of Rome, God's people, "Come out of her, my people," so the people of God are there, just as everywhere God has people, whom he has regenerated by his spirit. You see I look upon a Christian not as a relationship to a church, or even to a creed, but his relationship to Christ. What is a man's relationship to Christ? Is Christ Lord of his life? That's why I wear a wee badge; Christ is Lord because I believe that that is the root thing, that there is a personal relationship with the Son of God.

TERRY WYNN: You've always fought for Ulster to remain part of the United Kingdom...

IAN PAISLEY: That is the relationship of course...

TERRY WYNN: ...is that purely a political decision or is that to do with faith?

IAN PAISLEY: No, it's to do with the Reformation and the Revolution Settlement and the Protestant succession. But that doesn't mean that I would not be a Christian if there was no Revolution Settlement. I mean it's just the way it is in history, just the same as it is with, in the same way as your own Methodist Church coloured a lot of Labour history. I mean I've heard a lot of people say, though it came from other places, but the real old-fashioned Kier Hardie stuff was real Methodist stuff.

TERRY WYNN: I mean the Labour party got more from the Methodism than they ever did from Marxism. I mean the beginnings of it were all good non-conformist.

IAN PAISLEY: No doubt about it. And then they were dedicated to do something for the working classes.

TERRY WYNN: Absolutely

IAN PAISLEY: Absolutely. I mean the working classes knew that they had a voice, and it became the voice of the working classes.

TERRY WYNN: How do you view politics in this day and age in Westminster and here, where there's so much secularism?

IAN PAISLEY Well, I think it's very sad. I think it's very sad that...Christians are not witnessing to their faith. I mean I don't like the attitude of a man who will whisper "I am a Christian", but when it comes to political matters doesn't want to be labelled as a Christian. I mean there is a reproach in being a Christian. And I mean Christ was reproached, and Christ said that you will suffer if you... the world, I mean the world doesn't like Christ. The world is an anti-Christ in many ways. A Christian is a person that brings his Christianity to bear on the situations he deals with, and if he does that in the way that he should do it—in likeness to Christ, then there's a very great loss, because it is a good thing to champion need, but better to champion need if you've love in your heart. And it's according to motivation...I mean if I'm only a good constituency worker because I want to keep my seat, then I think that is not what I should be. I think I should be a good constituency worker because I'm a Christian, you know.

TERRY WYNN: Is it possible to have good in your heart and not be a Christian?

IAN PAISLEY: It is, but not saving good. I mean I would distinguish between goodness...I mean you could be...I could be a pauper and ask you for half a crown (laughs) old money, and you would give me it, if you could find half a crown. But the point is this here: that is not saving faith. I mean I distinguish between saving faith and faith that conforms to law. You can conform to the law and not have saving faith. You see I think the difference where we would part ways would be that my emphasis would be more on a personal...relationship to Christ. I mean, I don't think that the church...I mean the Lord's not going to say to me when I get to heaven "I want to see your label." He wants to see my relationship to His Son. And I think that's the big thing, I think that gets us above church barriers, gets us above that whole thing, and we take Christianity where it should be, it is an allegiance to the Son of God, and allegiance to the only true God, and his Son Jesus Christ. And when you have that relationship then that should motivate you to do the things you ought to do, but I mean that ...I expect a Christian to tell the truth, therefore I expect a politician to tell the truth. And I think that that is perhaps very hard for politicians to do in a crooked age. But you have to do it.

TERRY WYNN: If when you got to heaven and God said: "Look at all the bleeding problems that you've caused down there; all the trouble, you know, all the strife," how would you answer that?

IAN PAISLEY: Well, I'd have to say that to His Son who came not to send peace but a sword, to turn the mother-in-law against her father-in-law and so on. I mean Christ was a troublemaker—did it not say of him, that he led sedition through the whole country? So then you said...

TERRY WYNN: Is that how you counteract the accusation when people say that's all you do is cause trouble?

IAN PAISLEY: Yes, people would say to you: "Look at the language you use," I mean I never use anything as picturesque as Christ's language, "generation of vipers." I didn't say to these people, "You're a lot of owd snakes." I mean, I mirror myself upon Christ, my faith is a personal allegiance to him, therefore, my prayer life, which is very essential, is a personal communication with him. I communicate with God through Jesus Christ. I want to be like Christ. But you see, Christ wasn't a sort of soft-voiced sissy that walked round Palestine. Christ was a furious man. I mean how many pulpits would accept Christ into them today? If he came into the crypt of Westminster Abbey today, would the House of Commons allow him to use it?

TERRY WYNN: The accusations of demonisation, that's your answer to it, when people accuse you.

IAN PAISLEY: Yes, well that of course and also I guess, they don't know me, I mean people who accuse me don't know me and don't know my way. For instance, I was walking outside Westminster the other day and a woman stopped me, and she said: "I have five children with me, and I want all my children to shake hands with you." And I said: "Why?" and she said: "I'm an Ulster Roman Catholic, but you're a man I admire, and I tell my children, "Mr Paisley's a strong man, but he's a kind man.""

TERRY WYNN: Whenever you're seen on a TV screen, with a microphone in front of you, you come across as this aggressive character, against the Northern Ireland Agreement, against the Roman Catholic church, against the Republic of Ireland, and all this...where does the love fit into all that?

IAN PAISLEY: If a man's house is on fire, I don't walk in and say, "Now boys, let's open all these doors. Let's be very careful that we don't offend this fella', but let's get him out unburnt." I bring him out, and if my method is getting him out, and I do get people out, then I have to stick to that, and it works.

TERRY WYNN: But the point I'm trying to make is that as a politician, a Christian politician, and if the base of Christianity is about love, and about loving God, and about loving Jesus, how do you...

IAN PAISLEY I don't think that the press want to portray me as I am...They want me to be portrayed so that they will paint the picture. I mean, even Wesley himself was very strong against the Pope. He said things against the Pope that I have never said. I'm a sort of neutral! I mean, people will get that. I mean, I think that's part of the price. People said that about the Lord, in touch with Satan and so on, I mean if they called the master of the house Beelzebub, what will they not call his servants. I think that's part of the comments you have to take.

TERRY WYNN: Is there any time when you ever see Ulster being part of a United Ireland?

IAN PAISLEY: Well I don't, I'm not...

At this point the telephone rang. It sounded like reception telling him that he had a visitor. Unfortunately they were telling him in French. "Do you speak English, friend?" he asked, and it was left for Ian Paisley Junior to sort out.

TERRY WYNN: The question was, is there ever a time when you see Ulster being part of a United Ireland?

IAN PAISLEY: Well, it could be but I don't think it will be, because as far as the birth thing is concerned, I mean I've been hearing that since I was a child: "That when you're 25, Ian, there'll be no Northern Ireland." That's nonsense. The Roman Catholic people breed, so do the Protestant women breed as well, and I would say that today there is less large families among Roman Catholics, and there are larger families among Protestants. When I started my ministry 57 years ago, the average family of a protestant was two, a boy and a girl. If they got a boy and girl, that was a gentleman's family and that was all they could bring up properly. But in the Roman Catholic Church, there were so many that they had to be almost dragged up. But I mean the Roman Catholic people don't have that sort of problem today.

TERRY WYNN: How do we get an answer to the troubles in Northern Ireland then? I don't mean unification, I mean Ulster existing as part of a United Kingdom.

IAN PAISLEY: Yes, I think the answer to it is to leave it to Ulster men, and you English, you Labour men, you Hibernians or whoever you are, let the Ulster people.

TERRY WYNN: But what do you mean by that?

IAN PAISLEY: I believe that the Ulster people should be given charge of their own peace process.

TERRY WYNN: But isn't that what they were trying to do?

IAN PAISLEY: No, no, they did not, they said "No, we're going to have a peace process in which we're going to make the minority equal with the majority. And we're going to balance up weighted majorities, the leeway." You can't do that. Ulster people … I have never sat at a table where I knew that what I was saying was going to be heeded, because I knew the British government would overrule it. I mean, we have to come, when I sit down with you if you're a nationalist, and I'm a Unionist, and you're not going to change your nationalism, and don't tell me nicely that you are, and I'm not going to change my Unionism, I don't need to say that. We've got to get a way whereby in regard to bread and butter issues...

(Ian Paisley's son enters to remind him he still has other appointments.)

IAN PAISLEY: So the point is that I feel very strongly that we should give the peace process into the charge of the Northern Ireland politicians.

TERRY WYNN: But how do you do that to keep the Nationalists onside though?

IAN PAISLEY Well, the nationalists will have to come onside, that's where they get their way, that's where...they shouldn't get their way, they've got to take their place at the table like everyone else...

TERRY WYNN: But if they don't have their way, then will they not start killing again and bombing?

IAN PAISLEY: Well they'll have to stop the killers. Someday you have to face up to facts, and facts are not being faced up to.

TERRY WYNN: Is Gerry Adams a Christian?

IAN PAISLEY: Well, he may profess to be a Christian, but you see again, defining Christianity the way I define it...

TERRY WYNN: But he would profess to have a faith, I take it?

IAN PAISLEY: Oh he's very, very devout he is, very high up in the church, they tell me. But there was a fellow, actually one of our leading journalists, who was a Roman Catholic, he was interviewing McGuiness the other day, and he says, "Mr McGuiness, you and I are both sincere and devout Roman Catholics, but there's one thing that I don't understand about you. How you can say you're a devout Roman Catholic and believe in murdering people, even your own people?" and McGuiness said, "Oh, well I am a victim of British injustice." That's not an argument.

TERRY WYNN: How do you stand up to the accusation that you support the Unionist violence makers?

IAN PAISLEY: Well, nobody believes that because they have threatened me, they have fired at me, they have taken me away from the streets and bombed the church. That is crazy, and if you read the UDA, and the UVF official organs, there's one bad man in Northern Ireland, and you're looking at him! I am painted as the worst, which I'm very happy to be.

TERRY WYNN But coming back to the solution..

IAN PAISLEY: We've got to come to terms with one another. I mean I have told John Hume, "John, you can get as many Westminster people to agree with you, but you can never make it stick." If I don't say "John Hume, I'm going with this," the majority of Protestants will not be going with it. And if you don't say, "I'm not going with this," the majority of nationalists will not either. Let's face it; don't give yourself a personal advantage, I say start and practise your ecumenism.

TERRY WYNN: Which politicians do you have most respect for in Northern Ireland?

IAN PAISLEY: Well, I would have a good personal relationship with John Hume, but I mean we differ on the big issues but I mean that doesn't matter, I mean we worked very well for the people here, we got them their Peace money, we did very well for them, and that was a joint effort.

TERRY WYNN: Yeah, I remember that well.

IAN PAISLEY: I mean that…we…John and I have always been friendly. John is certainly not well now, which is a pity, it is.

TERRY WYNN: Ian, that's been fascinating.

IAN PAISLEY: Good, Good.

So where does that leave your average Christian politician. "If I'm a politician and a Christian, then I'll be a Christian politician." That's certainly acceptable, but would his brand of politics be applicable and acceptable outside the confines of Ulster. The English look at Northern Ireland politics and politicians in amazement. They look at American politicians with condemnation, especially the overtly religious, and they look on their own politicians with distrust. In a secular age, how should the Christian be a witness for his faith to others? Is it just by acting in a Christian manner, whatever that may mean, or is it to openly display it like Ian Paisley?

One thing I really liked was when he said "Christ wasn't a sort of soft-voiced sissy." This echoes an excellent sermon I once heard the Rev Tim Hall preach in my own church in Standish. It was a Men's Sunday Service and Tim made the point forcefully that Jesus was a man's man, someone with guts, prepared to take on injustice, stand up to the authorities, knock the establishment and display bravery beyond imagination. He was a real prophet in the Jim Wallis sense and yet he is invariably portrayed as the old Sunday School hymn states as "Gentle Jesus, meek and mild."

The interesting thing is that Ian Paisley grasps this tough image and reflects it in his policies. Is he to be condemned or praised for that?

Some years ago on a balmy summer evening, Doris and I were sat with John and Paulette Tomlinson in the Grande Place in Brussels. John was a colleague of mine at the time, later to go to the House of Lords.

As we chatted a bloke passing by recognised John and came over for a chat, sat down and enjoyed a drink with us. He was from the Social Democratic Party of Sweden and knew John from a long time back.

He was good company, spoke reasonably good English and was quite chatty. Things were going well until he began to tell us of where he lived and the nearby lake with its colony of swans. "They come there for the f—ing, it is famous for the f—ing that swans do" he said as four jaws dropped and laughter was stifled because we all knew he meant the word 'breeding'. After about ten "f—ings" he moved the conversation away from the lake and the swans. Not one of us corrected him and when he went we all burst into laughter. Should we have told him? Can you imagine him making a public speech in English and telling a British audience all about the swan breeding near where he lives.

At what point do you say to someone, you need to change what you are saying because it is potentially offensive? Do you say it to politicians? Do you say it to Christians? Too often we don't say to others we think you are wrong, we are too embarrassed to correct them.

But what if they are told and they keep their version and don't change as I'm sure Ian Paisley has been told time and time again. Now I know there is a big difference between a Swede getting his words wrong and what faith-led politicians say, but when do we know if they are right or not?

I have a poster in my office: "If you were arrested for being a Christian, would there be enough evidence to convict you." That says a lot, but after interviewing the 'Big Man', one could ask what type of evidence do you need?

EIGHT

The first time I met Paul Petrie was in my office in Brussels. He'd asked for an appointment and came to talk about the annual European Prayer Breakfast, which he and some colleagues helped to organise. The first one had take place in Brussels, but outside of the European Parliament. It was attended by political figures, ambassadors, European officials, NATO officials and politicians from national parliaments. The guest speaker had been Georgina Dufoix, a former French government Minister. I knew nothing about it, so when Paul came to see me to talk about holding such future gatherings within the Parliament, I began pumping him with questions. Who are you? Who are your colleagues? Who do you work for? How are you funded? My "beware" antenna went up as this American (actually he is Canadian, Rebecca, his wife, is American, and the States is where most of his fundraising for his NGO takes place) began to speak. I had visions of the American far right fundamentalists invading Europe, with me being in the middle of it. What would the UK press make of this?

In that sense I am no different from the average Brit, who gazes in amazement at how the Americans mix their politics quite openly with religion. It may be done for electoral reasons (as Tony Hall illustrates in Chapter 6), or it may just be that the Americans are not as reserved as the British and Europeans at talking openly about religion, faith and their personal beliefs. Whatever it is, it isn't what we are used to. (During the third Bush/Kerry Presidential televised debates in October 2004, the question master asked them both explicitly about the role their faith played in their political lives. Both had no problem in responding openly. Such a scenario is virtually impossible to imagine in the UK or in Europe generally).

But Paul was likeable, reassuring and convincing, so it was hard to resist not helping. The event took place in the European Parliament and Dagfinn Høybraten, the Norwegian Minister of Health, was the main speaker. It was good and has continued to be good each successive year.

The European Prayer Breakfast (EPB) is a mini version (actually a micro-version, 250 participants as opposed to 7000 in the States) of the National Prayer Breakfast that occurs in Washington D.C. in February each year. Paul, with connections to the Washington event, as someone living in Brussels, joined with other Christians to establish the EPB for European decision-makers. Since then, others have been established in various European capitals within their Parliaments.

Paul came from a non-Christian home and at the age of sixteen "had an encounter with God." His father wasn't best pleased and never came to terms with Paul becoming a Christian. Paul knew nothing about Jesus or the church and set about finding out. It was not until he went to university that he could freely, comfortably and openly discuss with other Christians. It was at university that he met Rebecca.

They married when they were both 21. Within days they were in the Congo as missionaries. As Rebecca said, for someone who had hardly been away from home before, this came as quite a shock. Not long after their arrival, they were caught up in the bloody conflict that the Congo of the sixties is remembered for. But they weren't deterred and after the trouble had subsided they returned.

Since 1985 they have been based in Brussels, running the European operation of the charity they work for. Both are about my age. Paul has had several mild heart attacks and strokes, which never seem to slow him down, and Rebecca has suffered from ME for some years now.

On the 4th October, 2001 she was having a coffee-morning gathering at her home when she fell down the stairs and broke her neck. Luckily one of the ladies was able to do whatever needed to be done to ensure she was still alive when the ambulance arrived, otherwise she would have been dead. The initial assessment of her condition was that she would be paralysed from below the neck on a permanent basis. Her lungs were paralyzed for the first several months and she was on a respirator. She had also had her vocal chords damaged and couldn't talk. This was the same type of damage the Superman actor Christopher Reeves had suffered, where only 1% survive.

They may not have much in way of money, but what they do have is a great family and a lot of friends around the world who began praying for her. I went to see her after about three months. She was still in intensive care, where she was for about five months. Paul did the lip reading so I could understand what she was saying. I did comment to her that during the 20 minutes I was there she had never stopped talking, which her great sense of humour appreciated. But the good news at that time was that she had feeling in her toe and in her left fingers.

Some months after when Doris and I went to see her, she had come on in leaps and bounds, metaphorically speaking of course. She could talk with a faint voice, feed herself with her left hand and had begun to keep a diary, writing with her left hand. She had been stood upright and commenced therapy for her legs when it was discovered that her head was not connected to her spine correctly. This meant having to stop all therapy and going to London for two operations to correct the problem, which involved inserting two screws via her mouth. It needed £20,000 to pay for it, which friends quickly got together. When we saw her she said, "I should have been dead three times according to the doctors. I'm not scared of death, but God must have some purpose for me."

Since then she has made great progress. Paul sends out regular updates, which I'm sure will one day make a wonderful book. There are about 5,000 people praying for her thanks to the power of e-mails. And if you want evidence that prayer works, you needn't look any further.

After 18 months in hospital she came home permanently on 11th April, 2003. Those regular updates he calls 'Rebecca's Journey' and to read them is to experience real faith shining through both Paul and Rebecca. I once asked Paul did he ever ask why it had happened, to which he replied, he'd never had the time to ask.

Paul would see one of his tasks as being a support for politicians, enabling them to meet other Christians and having the opportunities to share in fellowship together. Whatever my initial suspicions, I came to love both Paul and Rebecca. What follows are extracts from some of those 'Rebecca's journeys'; the problem was deciding what to leave out.

During the drafting of this book when it was being proof-read, I was told this chapter you are reading now didn't fit. It's a good read, a wonderful story but for a separate book.

So I read it and re-read it, shortened it a little more but decided it was staying in because what I want to show is how two people, who have dedicated their lives to helping others, live out their faith. It shows not only their continual thankfulness but their fears and doubts through an array of emotions.

If politicians want to put a Soul into societies then they need to have this kind of faith to move the immovable. When the question is asked "Where are the prophets?" these two people are not simply the kind who demonstrate or give to charity or do good works, they **are the ones** who have actually worked with the poorest and oppressed, dedicating their lives to them because they considered it to be God's work that needed to be done.

Paul's NGO is still working in Africa but also in trying to reconcile Palestinian and Israeli people. He helps to bring politicians of faith together. Thanks to him I came to know and befriend the likes of Boris Trajkovski and Tunne Kelan, both of whom have had an influence on me.

Remember Cedric Mayson's comments in my chat with Father Nolan, when he said that people of faith who get into politics can easily "get caught up in promoting the political policy," he said they need to take time out to reflect as a group. That is exactly what Christian MEPs do when we meet each month in Strasbourg. It's a real sharing, something I look forward to. It's something that Paul had promoted and it's worth including this section in this book if only to see the type of people he and Rebbeca are.

Whilst it may seem lengthy, it's worth reading if you want an insight into what true belief can do to individuals, especially under such circumstances.

Greetings, Friends,

On the anniversary of September 11 I wrote some thoughts that I'd like to share with you now.

"Today is 9.11. I just arrived home and turned on the BBC. It is Remembrance Day! Like most of us, I remember where I was when the Twin Towers were struck—Rebecca and I were in Kinshasa. The cell phone rang. It was Mary, my secretary, asking if we had heard what was happening. We had not. She began describing, live, what she was watching on CNN. I was gripped with a certain horror, and surrealism. As the day progressed we travelled across town to the home of friends who had access to CNN. Glued to the events, watching with incredulity, our senses rejecting the reality we were seeing, there was the knowledge that the world, as we had known it, was changing. In many ways, October 4 was, for us, a reliving of 9.11. It was the day our lives were changed—the day of Rebecca's accident. As I called each of our children from the hospital that day, there were similar emotions of incredulity and surrealism, a similar visceral rejection of the reality into which we had just been plunged, and the same sense: life will permanently change because of this event.

America has gone on, and faced the processes of recovery with hope and determination. Our family, likewise, has gone on, with the determination to hold to the One who is the source of hope.

Many things have changed for us. The wife and mother who is so central to our lives, hasn't been in our home for a year. Her function has certainly changed. But some things haven't changed. First and foremost, the love and goodness of God, rooted in His good and loving character, haven't changed. My, and our, love for Rebecca has only deepened. Though she is not here in our home, she is still central to our lives, and home is where she is.

Yesterday, in the hospital, I said to her: "Whatever it holds, the future will be good, and we'll face it together with anticipation." It will be a different kind of "good" than we had imagined, but good nonetheless. There is a song that says: 'God is good, all the time.' That can be construed as superficial and unrealistic—or it can be the testimony of eternal reality. In our minds and lives, the latter is true. He is indeed good—all the time.

One year on from Rebecca's accident, we want to thank God for His faithfulness and goodness. Our focus is on the future. We find joy in the One who is our life. The same power that raised Jesus from the dead, that brought His broken, lifeless body surging back from the grave, is the life that also lives in Rebecca. We pray that that same power will surge into her physical body, continuing the restoration process. We "wait in hope."

I want to close with a passage from Colossians 1 that has become a reality in us: "We pray that you'll have the strength to stick it out over the long haul—not the grim strength of gritting your teeth, but the glory-strength that endures the unendurable and spills over into joy."

Our love to you all,
Paul

★ ★ ★ ★

1 November 2002

Greetings, Friends,

Rebecca's chronic fatigue has flared up again, so the doctors are reducing her therapy to two sessions a day for the next while. Rebecca and I have both experienced some discouragement with this.

Arrangements have been made for Rebecca to make a trip home—the first for 13 months. On Saturday, 16 Nov., the ambulance will bring her home for the day. We'll have a hospital bed set up in the dining room, and a fire in the fireplace. A nurse will come several times during the day to do the nursing "things" that need to be done. We're also planning for another couple of weekends at home before Christmas, and then five days over Christmas. The family will all be together. It is good for Rebecca to have things like this to look forward to and to plan toward.

★ ★ ★ ★

24 November, 2002

Greetings, Friends,

Yesterday we had a mini-milestone. When Rebecca was put in her wheelchair she said, for the first time, that it felt good to be up. That may seem small, but it is a significant step. Some background: When a patient has been immobile and prone for long periods (and Rebecca was five months in ICU, in addition to the subsequent hospitalization) the blood vessels loose their elasticity and are not able to keep blood in the upper parts of the body; this, in addition to metabolic changes, makes sitting up most difficult. In Rebecca's case this results in nausea, etc. So, for sitting up to actually feel good, even for the first few moments, is a long way from where she has been in months past.

★　★　★　★

Dear Friends,

This is Paul. It's Monday afternoon, and I'm at the hospital. We had a wonderful 30 hours at home with Rebecca over the weekend. We began decorating for Christmas. Stephen was the motor behind this, with Rebecca giving suggestions from her bed, surrounded by boxes of decorations and pine bows. Sunday brunch was Rebecca's first meal at table in over 14 months. We wheeled her chair to a beautifully decorated Christmas table, looking out over the garden. Stephen fixed omelettes and other goodies. She says she's not ready for a fancy restaurant yet (true-smile!), but it is another real step forward.

She has had several thoughts that she wanted to share with you, so I'll take dictation.

~One of the recent wonderful developments that I've experienced is the ability again to read my Bible for myself. My nurses prop it up with pillows and help me get my reading glasses on. One nurse always drops a tissue into my hand and quietly closes the door. Last Sunday morning I was reading in Matthew, the Sermon on the Mount, (one of those passages we've all read many times). When I got to the part: "He who saves his life will lose it, but he who loses his life for My sake will find it," it was as if I'd never read it before. I have lost a life, in His service, and, in the coming months, will surely be finding a new life, in His good plan and purpose. My mind immediately went to Paul's and my discussion, just days before, about the possibility of a new bedroom on our house. This was really the first time I had been able to envision a place for me in the future.

The next day, when the doctors made their rounds, they talked, for the first time, about my working toward going home every weekend, with the goal of going home permanently by the spring. It was a bit of a shock to me. And then I remembered "finding a new life," and such joy filled my heart. Isn't His Word, and the timing of it, amazing? His kindness and goodness continually catch up with me and overwhelm me.

I've had another unfolding story this past month. It began when a new student nurse leaned over my bed and a silver cross gleamed out from her uniform. I said to her: "Does that cross have meaning for you, or is it just a lovely piece of jewellery?" "Oh," she said, "It has meaning—and I'm supposed to find out if you are a believer." I was so shocked! In the discussion that followed she disclosed that another student had become suspicious of my faith by some of the Bible verses written around my room. She had said to Natalie: "You find out if she is a believer. My English isn't good enough."

What followed has been a most delightful, daily sharing of the Lord's life with Natalie, who, I came to find out, was a brand new believer. She is in the process of leading her two teenage children toward the Lord.

Some weeks ago I asked Paul to get several Flemish New Testaments, a new translation. So on Natalie's last day here I gave the first NT away. I pointed her to Matt. 11:28–30, ("Come unto Me all you who are weary..."). She immediately went off by herself with her NT, only to come back in 15 minutes, tears streaming down her face. She said: "How did you know what I needed? God has spoken to me!" I just said: "Natalie, go to Jesus, and He will lead you to the Father."

What a daily adventure we are all having together; as you pray, Jesus is leading. I still have three more NTs. Won't it be fun to see who they are for?

Love from us both,

Paul & Rebecca

*   *   *   *

Greetings, Friends,

One additional prayer request: For the past 37 years Rebecca and I have created our life together, partnering not only in the raising of our children, but in all that we've done and initiated. We've worked and traveled together, and our life has unfolded out of our relationship and communication. Rebecca's present limitations create a new situation. My desire and commitment is that the life ahead of us will proceed out of our relationship just as the life behind us has. We, frankly, don't know how to do this. Rebecca will be moving home in about six weeks. We're making the preparations for that now. I don't want to go about my life and just "visit" her regularly in her room. We need wisdom and insight to know how to create our future together.

★   ★   ★   ★

Greetings, Friends,

From Rebecca:

One of the lovely things about the way the Father works in our lives is that He leads us, step by step, through the processes that we need. Coming home from Pellenberg last weekend, we came around the round-about at the little lake where Paul and I walked for many years. My mind went back to our walks, to eating together in some of the restaurants that circle the lake, and I felt sad. I carried that sense of sadness through the evening. The next morning in my quite time the Lord brought it back to mind, and gently rebuked me. He reminded me of the Scripture: 'He who puts his hand to the plow and looks back is not worthy of the Kingdom.' Surely there is an important place in our lives for remembering, with thanksgiving, but when that remembering turns to a longing for what is past, it can become sin. I was given the precious gift of repentance. I wept, realizing that the Lord desired for me to look ahead and not back. What has been, has been His gift to me, but no more so than that which is ahead. That too is His gift to me. I'm reminded of the Scripture in Jer. 29:11 "For I know the plans I have for you," declares the lord, "plans to prosper you and not to harm you, plans to give you hope and a future."

★ ★ ★ ★

Dear Friends,

We are now less than two weeks until Rebecca comes home permanently. What a day that will be! After 18 months in 5 different hospitals, five major surgeries, innumerable minor procedures and crises, we will celebrate her homecoming. God has been so faithful and so good.

Yesterday we had a milestone event: Rebecca's first outing. Robert and Tracy had us over to their home for an afternoon English Tea (Tracy is English). As you know, they live directly across the street. Robert and Stephen carried her up the stairs in her wheelchair to their lovely new premises. The table was beautifully set with snowy white Belgian lace and lovely china. Tracy fixed cucumber sandwiches, lemon cake, biscuits, and truffles, served in a tiered silver serving piece, with classical music playing and good fellowship. It was a luxurious hour sipping fine English tea—a good beginning for future outings. On the way back home some of the neighbours came out and waved to Rebecca. They were glad to see us out and about.

From Rebecca: 'Give thanks in all things, for this is the will of God in Christ Jesus concerning you' (I Thes. 5:17). Years ago Paul told me that the Greek here means to 'cover all things with the umbrella of thanksgiving.'

I'm always amazed at how I can forget lessons that, over the years, the Lord has made a part of the very foundation of my walk with Him. This week I made a discovery of just such an area.

I've been having what to me is a noticeable change in my left hand (my good hand). I seem to have less control, although my mobility is still good. When I talk to the doctors about it, they can't see much of a change. And besides, they don't know what to do about it, since they don't know why I can use my left hand anyway.

This week the Lord showed me that I was worrying about it. Over 30 years ago the Lord taught us to exchange worry for thanksgiving. John Wesley said: 'I would rather curse and swear than worry.' It has been such a joy to live a life full of thanksgiving, knowing that the God of love was in control, and was sending good things. But in these last weeks worry has crept in. I was worried about my left hand! I asked the Lord to forgive me, and decided that every time I noticed any change, I would thank Him and praise Him for His goodness (and for your prayers). I am covered, and I am His. I'm so thankful that we are able to be a people whose hearts are full of thanksgiving and gratitude."

Our love to you all,
Paul and Rebecca

★　★　★　★

Dear Friends,

This is Wednesday, April 16. Rebecca's nurse just left. We have an hour before the physical therapist arrives, and wanted to use this time to get a note off to you all. Rebecca's transition home has been full of grace and joy. Words just aren't adequate to express the delight in having her home again permanently.

I'll let Rebecca tell you herself about the transition: "I think each morning when I wake up, it is still hard for me to realize that I'm now living at home, and not at the hospital. There were teary good-byes to my nurses, who had prepared some lovely surprises for me. I trust we'll be able to have a few of them here for lunch in the not-too-distant future. As I was leaving the hospital, I was struck by the difference in my capacities now, compared to 12 months ago when I first arrived in Pellenberg. I am able to eat quite well by myself, drink from a regular glass, brush my own teeth, write legibly, hold and dial a phone, manage a remote control, turn the pages of a book, and even take my medications by myself. About three weeks ago I began again to sketch and do watercolour. It certainly isn't what it used to be, but I wasn't discouraged with the results, and look forward to continuing this. (This is an insert from Paul: I thought her work, especially the second painting of two little birds, was great.) These may seem like simple things, but since you know where I've come from, they are major accomplishments. I'm so thankful for each step toward independence, however small.

Yesterday I was reading in Luke 5 where the friends of the paralytic lowered him on a mat down through the roof to Jesus. It says that when Jesus saw their faith, He said: "Friend," and healed him.

As many of you know, this week is another intensive prayer initiative for us, leading up to Easter. I saw myself as the paralytic, and you as my friends, carrying me to Jesus. The picture deeply touched me, and I'm resting on the mat of your faith and love.

I think this is especially significant in this week of transition from being in the hospital to being at home. It was a bit wrenching to leave Pellenberg, having been there for so long, with the security of nurses and doctors around the clock. This week has been the beginning of working with our new "team": a nurse who comes twice a day, and a physiotherapist who comes once a day. The physio is excellent, and working me hard. But, of course, it is such a joy to be awakened every morning by my beloved Paul, and surrounded by my family and friends. Annie is here with us for a month, and that is always a delight.

I said to Paul yesterday: 'It is a whole new life. Who, at 58, has the opportunity to start over?' God is so good, and I am blessed, in them and in you."

Paul again: Continuing Rebecca's last thought, on the first evening of her homecoming, kneeling by her bed, I said to her that this is the first day of the rest of our lives. We're together starting a new phase of life, under the careful oversight of the Lover of our souls. We stand with expectation to see what He will do.

Our love to you all,

Paul & Rebecca

★ ★ ★ ★

Greetings, Friends,

From Rebecca: "I think it was most significant that the special prayer week was during my first week home. You can imagine that, as thrilled as I am to be here, the week was one of adjustments. I felt the natural insecurity of being without my doctors and nurses. For 18 months I only had to press a button for any medical care that I might need. One of my hardest mornings was when I woke up feeling an overwhelming sense of my limitation, as well as the pain of feeling that my need for constant care must be a burden to my family and friends. When Paul came back down after our quiet-times to have breakfast with me, I began to cry, saying: 'I can't imagine spending the rest of my life like this. How can I do this?' He listened to me, and then quietly said: 'One day at a time!' Such a load lifted from me, because that's what Father has promised grace for—one moment at a time. Since then there has been a joy in awakening in His presence, wondering what He has planned for that day."

★ ★ ★ ★

Greetings, Friends,

Rebecca: I've been home now about six weeks, and, as you know, it is wonderful to be here with my dear family and loved ones. Needless to say, there have been adjustments for everyone, and often those adjustments have not been easy. We've each felt stretched in different ways, and have appreciated your prayers.

Twice my afternoon naps have turned a bit challenging. I use the base of a cordless phone as my call system. The person responsible for me has the receiver, and when I need them, I push the "phone finder" which rings in the receiver. On two different occasions the base unit has slipped beyond my reach.

It isn't entirely rational. I could hear my dear family tiptoeing overhead and whispering in the hallway. I knew they were so glad I was getting such a long nap. But I flashed back to the old days at ICU when I was unable to communicate or call for help. I ended up with an overwhelming sense of my complete vulnerability and inability.

On the morning of the first afternoon, in my quiet time, the Lord had spoken to me through the Psalms that He was ever watching, and that He heard my cry. That afternoon, after about 45 minutes of not being able to get anyone's attention, I began to cry. Then I remembered the Psalm, but, I'm sorry to say, it didn't help me much at the time. I felt the old panic of isolation and fear. About that time, Judy stuck her head around the corner to check on me. Then I really cried!

The second time this happened, about three weeks later, I did better, more able to hold on to the reality that the Lord was watching me, and knowing that He would soon send someone to me. I think the end result of both experiences drove home the reality of my incapacity and my dependence. My care, my life, really requires a team. We're coming to see that it is an expression of His Body—His life expressed in and through our relationships.

Paul again: Rebecca's statement that our life requires a team effort is a reality for us all. The Father created us for dependence on Him and interdependence with the community of which we are a part. Thank God for people and relationships.

This week Rebecca's physical therapist discovered that she had new movement in her right leg. She said it is continuing enervation.

Our love to all,

Paul & Rebecca

★   ★   ★   ★

Whatever the circumstances, there is always reason for hope and confidence. Life is so different from what Rebecca and I had imagined it would be. And in the midst of loss we have found great treasure. In the midst of change we have discovered more deeply the wonders of the One who never changes.

The future is not found looking back. Longing for things as they were makes the present good insipid. David said: "I would have perished if I had not believed to see the goodness of God in the land of the living."

We have found the goodness of God in the land of the living, and look forward every day to what He will show of Himself, and what He will do.

As always, many thanks for standing with us on this journey.

Our love to all,
Paul

★   ★   ★   ★

Rebecca's Up-date: July 14, 2003
Dear Friends,

When we first started writing updates to you, Paul and I determined that we wanted to be candid about the challenges and our responses to them. We wanted to express the reality of our day-by-day happenings, both in our circumstances and in our souls. Today I am very discouraged. I am better than I was earlier this morning, and will be better by this evening, I'm sure. I had a good cry with Judy, or should I say we had a good cry together. I also had a good time with the Lord, so my perspective is a bit better.

I especially want to share these thoughts with those of you who have serious or extended illness. Yesterday and today I have felt a terrible burden, or should I say I have felt that I am a terrible burden to everyone around me. The reality is that everything I need must be brought to me or done for me. Often I don't even express the things I want because there are so many things I need. To "want" something only adds more of a burden to those who love me and are committed to my care. Everyone around me needs a break to get away from me. I know it is not a break from me, but a break from the burden of my constant care.

Judy expressed it well this morning when she said: "He is faithful to bring us all to a place where we know we need Him. We can't do it on our own." She, in her extremity and weariness, sometimes not knowing if she can go on, and me in my inability to continue being so needy, wanting to get up and do something for myself. The Lord has to teach us how to do this. All along, and especially lately, my cry has been: "Lord, teach me, show me. I don't know how to do this. Teach me how to go through the day as You would go through it." It is in our extremity that we truly find Him.(How many times have I said this to you?)

★ ★ ★ ★

Dear Friends,

Greetings from sunny Europe, where the heat has been record-breaking for several weeks. Oh for air-conditioning!

Susannah and my cousin, Diane, from Toronto, arrived several days ago. They've been a real help to Annie and me, and a joy to have in our home. Of course Stephen, Robert, and Tracey are in Congo for a month.

From Rebecca: "Release has been an important part of every area of my life. In no place have I felt it more keenly than in relation to our children. It's funny that we have to release them into the Hand of God as if they were ours, and not His, in the first place.

I remember when our Matthew was a teenager, and I was needing to release him. I was struggling, and the Lord said to me, 'I'm praying for him.' What a relief!

Then when we left Susannah at university for the first time, on the way home we cried, and reminisced, and cried, and reminisced some more. After we got home, I was fine. People said to me that they were surprised that I was not having more of an adjustment to my only daughter being away from home. I realized that leaving her and releasing her to university was not so difficult because I'd been releasing her her whole life.

Several weeks ago, our Phillip was home for a short time. He sat on my bed and we laughed and prayed together. It was one of the sweetest times we'd ever had. Then he had to leave to return to North America to begin his university. I got to leave him in the hands of the One who loves him more than his Daddy and I do.

All of this is so fresh in my mind because our "baby," Stephen, is in the Democratic Republic of Congo right now. He left, with Robert and Tracey, a week ago today, flying through London, Nairobi, Kigali, (Rwanda), then busing across the Congolese border to the eastern town of Goma, and flying in a Russian cargo plane across trackless jungle to Lodja. He called, via satellite phone, two days ago, to let us know they had arrived safely. In Stephen's inimitable fashion, when I asked how he was doing, he said: "Everything is grrreat!"

Two weeks ago Paul was in the States and I was struggling: 'We're going to send our baby, 17 years old, into a war zone. We've got to be crazy.' I struggled with it all night. Have you noticed that situations are always much worse in the middle of the night? In the morning I wakened, and said to the Lord: 'OK, if You don't change my mind by the time Paul gets home tomorrow, I'm going to say that this child cannot go to Africa. I have no peace about it.'

I went into my quiet time. These days I always begin in the Psalms. I was in Ps. 107, and the Lord said: 'No, not there.' I kept turning the pages until I got to Ps. 112. He said: 'There!' In verse 7-8 it says: 'He will have no fear of bad news; his heart is steadfast, trusting in the Lord. His heart is secure, he will have no fear; in the end, he will look in triumph on his foes. He has scattered abroad his gifts to the poor, his righteousness endures forever.' I realized that the thing I feared was bad news. And when I read about scattering our gifts to the poor, Stephen is a most precious gift, and Congo is the poorest of the poor. I knew that the Lord was in it, and that I could trust Him to bring about His purpose.

In the back page of my Bible, I have each of the children named with the Scriptures the Lord had given me in their growing up years. Each one represents a letting go. Maybe it is an acknowledgement of to Whom they really belong."

Love from us both, and many thanks for your prayers.

Paul and Rebecca

★ ★ ★ ★

Our Dear Friends,

On August 16th many of you joined together in a 24 hours prayer vigil for me. I would say that the results have been stunning.

My physiotherapist said, with tears in her eyes: 'I can't believe it! You have new movement in every limb. 'In my situation, one is not supposed to gain any new movement after the earlier stages of recovery. Now, two years later, for the first time, I'm able to hold my right foot in an upright position. I have new movement in my left thigh, which is beginning to enable me to pull my knee up. I'm able to move my left arm so that it touches the pillow above my head. My upper right arm is beginning to show movement. I'm able to sit unsupported on the side of the bed, and move left and right, backwards and forwards. It is all just beginning, but it is all evidence of increased re-enervation of neurological pathways. Every day is hard work, but I'm so encouraged by all of your prayers and support.

One day, when the nursing staff had changed again, and the cement mixer was pounding in my ears, and I was so tired, I cried out to the Lord and said: 'How can I live like this?' He reminded me: 'Thank me in all things' (I Thes. 5:18). Many years ago the Lord challenged Paul and me to not complain, but instead, to thank Him. Sometimes, in the big things, we remember to thank Him, but often forget in the daily frustrations and struggles. Covering every day with the umbrella of thanksgiving enables us to release circumstances into our Father's loving hands, and reach up and find Him, and receive His grace. He brings His joy and peace, even in the midst of pounding and confusion.

Paul and I once again thank you for standing with us.

All my love, Rebecca

And my love too,
Paul

★ ★ ★ ★

Dear Friends,

Thanks for your constancy in prayer. As we mentioned in the last e-mail, Rebecca is experiencing some concerning symptoms. The neurosurgeon ordered X-rays and an MRI. Those are now done, and we're waiting for the results. We'll let you know as soon as we hear from the doctors.

Rebecca: "Dear Ones, Paul is in such a busy season, but we realized that we wanted to communicate with you this week. We've shared each step along the journey. At first I found a hesitation in sharing the things that seemed negative, but that is part of our story. In recent months it has been progress and progress. During the last month, however, my condition has deteriorated. But our confidence is in Him, to see what He will unfold.

About two weeks ago I was having lots of spasticity, not having been able to do physiotherapy for several days because of it. I was experiencing increased numbness, and generally felt bad. I went down for my nap, but could not sleep. My mind went from one thing to another. At one point I thought about my scripture that morning in Ps. 37. In two different places it says: 'Do not fret.' My deteriorating physical situation had been a source of pressure for me. A rush of anxious thoughts flooded in upon me. Then I remembered the Ps.: 'When my anxious thoughts multiply within me, Your consolations delight my soul.'

I thought, 'Well Lord, console me!' He spoke, 'I will take care of you.' I immediately fell asleep. When I wakened after a good nap, Paul came down to tell me that he'd been able to talk directly to Professor Goffin, the neurosurgeon, and we had an appointment in two days.

Surely our lives are made of a series of seasons of confidence and rest, followed by waves of insecurity and pressure. Each one perfectly designed to press us back into the loving arms of the One who cares for us, more than we can ever comprehend.

We are grateful for these new stretching days, and for your prayers.

I must say this. Later that week, the morning of the MRI, He gave me Isa. 63:9: 'In all their distresses, He too was distressed, and the angel of His presence saved them. In His love and mercy He redeemed them; He lifted them up and carried them all the days of old.'

Do you remember when we were going to London for the surgeries? He gave me Deut. 33:12: 'The one the Lord loves rests between His shoulders.' Gee, we're being carried again. What will this next phase hold? We don't know, but we know Him, and we thank you that you're praying. We'll keep you informed."

Love from us both,
Paul & Rebecca

★　★　★　★

Greetings, Friends!

The other morning Paul walked through my room, and it came to me that I 'get to do' this thing called life with him. Suddenly it all came together in my mind. The incredible brevity of my life, of Paul's life, and that we get to live at the same time in history—together. And then I thought of Judy, and Josi, Annie, each of you, that in the divine purpose of God we are all here in this brief 'wink of an eye' at the same time to share the great adventure called life, in Him.

I've thought about it each day since. I hope it will stay with me through this year, that we will finish our task together, completing His purpose for us, and seeing what He will do this year, this 'wink of an eye'.

★　★　★　★

Greetings, Friends,

I have a personal health report to give. Rebecca's thoughts will follow, as they are related to this recent development.

I returned from an extended trip to North America on 12 February.

Rebecca and I had our first "date" since her accident, just the two of us, on Valentine's Day, the 14th. We celebrated the 40th anniversary of our engagement. On Monday, 16 February, en route into Brussels, I had a mini-stroke, followed by 2 more after I returned home. At my doctors' suggestion, I was taken to the hospital and admitted. The following day I had another episode, which left me with some limited movement in my left hand and droopiness on the left side of my mouth. Five days of extensive exams followed. The doctors were not able to definitely identify the source, but think that some blood had clotted in one of the upper chambers of my heart, and had broken loose, going to my head. Each episode resulted in short-term loss of speech capacity. That is behind me now.

I've been home from the hospital for about a week, and have cancelled my next several international trips, to both recover, and listen to the Lord.

While in the hospital I read Hebrews 12 again: "…let us run with perseverance the race marked out for us. Let us fix our eyes on Jesus, the author and perfecter of our faith… Consider Him…" Faith is what we live by, but He is the author and perfecter of that. Our job is to keep eyes, hearts and minds fixed firmly on Him, and to view all our circumstances through Him. I'm so grateful that the Father has made Jesus the centre of all things.

Rebecca: "As you can imagine, the events which Paul has just recounted were difficult for me. It is surely harder when the Lord allows our loved ones to be touched, than when He does the same for ourselves.

The evening that Paul spent in the ER, Tracy and Judy stayed with me. (Robert and Stephen were with Paul.) I had moments of weeping, and moments of rest and faith—vacillating between the two. The next morning as I awakened, it was such a sick feeling realizing that my beloved was in the hospital. I went to the Lord, and happened to be reading in Matt. 14. It is always a wonder to me that He is so faithful to meet us wherever we are. I came to verse 22: 'Jesus made the disciples get into the boat and go ahead of Him to the other side.' Later it says that the waves and wind were against them. He made them go into rough seas. Then He came walking to

117

them on those rough seas. When they saw Him, they didn't recognize Him and were 'terrified, "It's a ghost," they cried'. In the midst of the storm, in the midst of their fear, they couldn't see clearly. Verse 27 says: 'But Jesus immediately said to them: "Take courage! It is I. Don't be afraid."' When I read this, I was so touched by the fact that He made them go into the storm; He was in the storm. I realized once again that He was in our storm. Oh, how could I forget! 'Take courage! It is I. Don't be afraid.' With those words, such peace came to me, such quietness.

I thought of all of you, and what your storms might be, and prayed for you. 'Lord help us to see You in the storm, however great or small. When You are there, then I'm at peace."'

> Our love to you all,
> Paul

★ ★ ★ ★

Greetings, Friends!

Thanks to those of you who prayed for me after my stroke. I'm feeling much better, and have regained most of the use of my left hand. I cancelled all my international trips until August, and have a slower schedule, getting to bed early most nights. Little by little I can feel myself recovering from the demands of the last 30 months. It is wonderful to be home, enjoying the coming of spring.

From Rebecca: "We are so greatly blessed to be surrounded and carried as we are by your love and prayer. I want to report that, after the day of prayer on my birthday, April 4, we have seen some definite progress. From that day, my spasticity has been noticeably less. And I am beginning to have movement in my right hip joint. Just today, my physical therapist said: 'It's moving! This is just how the left leg began almost a year ago.' This is caused by nerve re-enervation. We are $2^1/_2$ years after the accident, and such a change as this is remarkable."

★ ★ ★ ★

There is a friend who comes every Monday morning to help care for Rebecca. Monique is originally from Mauritius, but has lived in Belgium many years and is married to a Brit. Several weeks ago Rebecca asked Monique if she would like to say something to those of you who get Rebecca's Journey. She said she would, so the following is from Monique:

"It takes a high dose of humility to agree to write a contribution to 'Rebecca's Journey'. I often wonder, after having read either Paul's or Rebecca's notes, what I could add, but I am writing as promised.

It's been over a year now since I met the Petries for the first time after having read about Rebecca's accident. I felt an urge to contact them and offer whatever help I could give a few hours a week.

How do you live with constant head pain, in fact so strong that it is sheer agony whenever the comb, or even a gentle finger, touches your scalp on the right side of your head and down to your ear? How do you cope with paralysis when you've been a most active servant of the Lord? How do you come to terms with the fact that you depend totally on other people for help with every aspect of the everyday things we take for granted, like brushing your teeth, getting washed, dressed, turning over to avoid bed sores? And when the pain reaches its peak, just when you thought it couldn't get any worse, and it does to the point of crying, how deep is your struggle?

And how do you react when your body has escaped your control, when you can't tell whether it is functioning as it should on a daily basis? I asked her the question once and she answered: 'I have learnt to shed layer after layer, a bit like the skins of an onion.'

I think I know the answer: Our Lord is actually using His beloved daughter, Rebecca, for His glory. He is at work in her and through her. I have seen the love which shines out of her that leaves me, and the many other people who are in touch with her, in no doubt.

I'm sure those who receive a handwritten note from her fully appreciate everything she puts in it: love, words of comfort, encouragement, congratulations. I watched her writing one recently,

119

when she finally could sum up enough energy and courage to do it—the sheer effort of writing (which is quite an organization in itself, as it takes 2 flat cushions, 1 writing support cushion, an anti-slip sheet, her specially designed pen, etc.). She was so physically drained after the effort that she had to lie still for some time.

I am the richer from my contact with Rebecca, and am still in the process of learning from her. It's hard to describe the life force that drives her. She is a tower of strength for the whole family and those who evolve around her. You can cry with her when the pain gets too strong, but most of the time she is ready to laugh, to cheer others up, to listen, and to enjoy whatever good thing the Lord sends her way.

Never in the course of this year have I seen her indulging in self pity. Rebecca is always asking everybody (including her nurses) about themselves, and is ready to sympathize when she feels one of them is going through a tough patch or to rejoice with those who share their joy with her.

If you can't find something in the house, the best person to ask is...Rebecca. She knows exactly where the little blue bottle with a red label can be found on the first shelf on the left in a particular cupboard. And if you haven't spotted it the first time, you had better look carefully (usually the thing is staring you in the face) because the little blue bottle is exactly where she says it is. How she knows beats me. The same goes for almost every item in every room on any floor of the house.

And please don't think that she just lets herself go because she is bedridden. If you have ever visited her, you would know what I am talking about. You should know that Rebecca prepared herself to welcome you and made efforts to look her best for you. This is a painstaking process of applying make-up (including all the necessary cosmetics—just give her left arm a gentle lift to help her reach the upper right side of her face). For me, who makes a real mess whenever I try to use mascara, it's a real wonder watching her apply the stuff on her eyelashes neatly. Once the lipstick is on, she's ready to proclaim: 'Don't I look dazzling now!' Who can compete with that? Not me, anyway.

I think this sums it up: She's dazzling, even with tears swelling in her eyes, dazzling with the light of Our Lord that shines through her. She is a blessing to all those who get to know her. Thanks, darling Rebecca!"

And thanks, Dear Monique!

For prayer: The last several weeks Rebecca has had a down-turn physically: substantially less energy, limited ability to be up in her chair, increased head pain, and diminished movement. We'd appreciate your prayers.

★　★　★　★

Having read through it again I'm glad I didn't omit it. I know this book is about faith and politics and the effects of faith on how politicians behave, but can you imagine if politicians (or people in general) could be so caring, trusting, faithful, thankful, honest and kind as the Petries are. I'm sure some would say we want our politicians to be tough, well they should ask themselves how easy do they think it has been for Paul and Rebecca. It certainly has been tough and they have gone through hard times and dark periods but still came through with a steadfast faith in the God they love.

★　★　★　★

During the first democratic elections in South Africa in April 1994, I was there as an official observer from the EU. I attended a briefing session that was being held and sat at a double desk where another observer was already sat. I had crept in a minute or so late and quietly sat down so there were no formalities or greetings.

I glanced around the room trying to take everything in whilst not trying to stare at my next door neighbour. I noticed his spectacles case on the desk and it had on it the address of the optician in Enniskillen. As the briefing went on I looked down the list of names and there was one G. Wilson. I knew immediately that I was sat next to Gordon Wilson, he was there as an Irish Senator, appointed to the Senate by the Irish Government even though he was a Northern Irish Protestant.

I had corresponded with him after reading Alf McCreary's book "Marie." He had written back and at the end of the meeting I introduced myself to him and we had a brief chat. I never saw him again but it was one of those moments in my life when I felt I had met someone really special and someone I had admired for almost seven years.

Sunday morning of the 8th November, 1987 was Remembrance Day throughout the UK. In the Northern Irish town of Enniskillen that day, as the townspeople gathered at the cenotaph the Irish Republican Army detonated a bomb that had devastating effects, killing and maiming many people. In the history of the troubles in Northern Ireland there had been many atrocities but this was the equivalent of bombing a congregation of worshippers at a church service. For those who can remember seeing the television coverage it was absolutely horrendous. The next day one of the survivors was interviewed, it was Gordon Wilson and his words resounded around the world and when I heard them, I cried.

He said, "The wall collapsed and we were thrown forward, rubble and stones all around us and under us. I remember thinking 'I'm not hurt' but there's a pain in my shoulder. I shouted to Marie, 'Are you alright?' and she said 'Yes'. She found my hand and said, 'Is that your hand, Dad?' I said 'Are you all right, dear?' but we were under six feet of rubble. Three or four times I asked her, she always said, 'Yes, I'm alright.'

I asked her the fifth time, 'Are you all right, Marie?' She said 'Daddy, I love you very much.' Those were the last words she spoke to me. I kept shouting 'Marie are you all right?' There was no reply. I have lost my daughter, but bear no ill will. I bear no grudge, dirty sort of talk is not going to bring her back to life. I don't have an answer but I know there has to be a plan. If I didn't think that, I would commit suicide. It's part of a greater plan and God is good and we shall meet again."

Gordon Wilson in those words epitomised what Christian love and forgiveness and compassion should be about. Where is the revenge, where the hate, where the cursing?

The world would indeed be a better place if everyone could have the faith and personality of that one man.

Of all the great and the famous people I have met it is people like the Petries and Gordon Wilson who gave me a glimpse of what heaven on earth could be like.

NINE

Members of the European Parliament were first elected in 1979, prior to that the European Assembly, as it was then called, had Members who were appointed by their national governments. One of that 1979 intake was Tom Megahy, a Scotsman who represented West Yorkshire. Tom tells the story that in those early days he went down to breakfast in his hotel and ended up sharing a table with a French Member. Both were monolingual and so no conversation could take place except for polite smiles and nods. However, as Tom was taking his seat he stretched out his hand to shake the hand of his new colleague and said in his Scots accent, "Tom Megahy." The Frenchman accepted his handshake with a smile and as Tom sat down he said, "Bon appetit." Pity there is no English equivalent, thought Tom.

Next day, same dining room, this time Tom is already seated when his French friend arrives. Tom beckons him to sit down and as he does so says to him "Bon appetit," to which the Frenchman responded "Tom Megahy."

A book could be written about such misunderstandings of language and culture, indeed some of the best stories in the Parliament concern interpretation gaffes. My favourite being the time that representatives from the old coal mining areas were lobbying the EU for funds. They were very successful and people from the UK, France, Germany, Belgium and Spain would get together to discuss their problems and strategies. On one occasion the British were meeting with the French and the French interpreter had to contend with an array of regional accents, Lancashire, Yorkshire, Welsh, Scots etc. She was doing okay until a little Geordie got up and in a broad North East accent said, "Ya know the trouble is in our part of the world, all the young lads have nay work and all they can do is go down to the woods every day badgerbaiting." Her interpretation came out as "A problem in our region is that the young men spend their time in the woods masturbating." And the French thought 'They have real problems in the North East.'

The great thing about learning a foreign language is that you don't just learn the language, you learn about the culture also. It's hard to dislike the French when you understand what makes them tick, yet many in the UK do (thanks to the Media).

Bear in mind that if you're a reader of the Daily Mail you end up disliking lots of people, not just the French. I once read an article by a former Mail journalist who said the editorial instructions were that readers had to feel angry after reading the story. But the Mail is not the only organ to peddle xenophobia.

As an aside, I often tell students never to automatically believe all they read in the papers, instead question events and seek the truth, since papers tell lies (no doubt they would say, "Just like politicians"). My favourite is when the *Mail* ran a story on the Parliament's pension scheme; I was on the Board of the Scheme and was quoted "Terry Wynn said yesterday," except it had been two years since I had spoken to the journalist who wrote it and over that two years it had a whole new context. When I contacted the Editor, he said, "A sub-editor's error, Mr. Wynn." They really should change their sub-editors.

Suspicion, disliking, hatred and often feelings of insecurity can come from ignorance of other people and their ways. In this day and age that applies for many people to Islam.

In Chapter One Cedric Mayson had suggested getting a cross-section of people of different faiths to interview. Cedric is very much involved in inter-faith work in his role as National Coordinator for the Commission for Religious Affairs, within the African National Congress (ANC).

In fact one of the most fascinating gatherings that Doris, my wife, and I attended was with Cedric in Johannesburg, with representatives of all faiths. The ANC give a lot of time in promoting multi-faith projects. In fact, how many mainstream political parties in Europe have religious affairs departments? The ANC are conscious of the dichotomy of having a wide variety of faiths and at the same time having big problems of criminality. So much so that they are working on a "Moral Renewal of the Nation" in an attempt to transform the ethics of society.

To give a few of quotes from their literature:

"When President Nelson Mandela asked to meet the religious leaders of South Africa in June 1997, he spoke of his concern *'for the spiritual health and vitality of our people. In our striving for political and economic development, the ANC recognises that social transformation cannot be separated from spiritual transformation.'*"

"Dr. Pixley Seme opened the first ANC Conference in 8 January 1912 with prayer and the singing of *'Nkoso Sikelele' (God Bless Africa).* The movement was based on a culture of high social and personal values, rooted in ubuntu, which were articulated repeatedly through the years of its growth."

As explained earlier the word UBUNTU, it means to be human, to value the good of the community above self-interest, to strive to help other people in the spirit of service, to show respect to others and to be honest and trustworthy.

"The battle to overcome oppression had a long history and encompassed many strategies of non-violent and armed struggle. The deep ethical content and spirit of the Freedom Charter, signed at Kliptown in 1955, made it not only a rallying cry for our own struggle, but a guide to many throughout the world. ANC President Chief Albert Luthuli received the Nobel Peace Prize for that same commitment."

"The ANC has consistently struggled for a culture of human rights which would accord respect and equality to all people irrespective of race, age, sex, colour or creed. *'No one is born hating another person because of the colour of his skin, or his background, or his religion,'* wrote Nelson Mandela. *'People must learn to hate and if they can learn to hate they can be taught to love, for love comes more naturally to the human heart than its opposite.'*"

"The African National Congress has a long history of association with the Church. Our founders were church men and women. Throughout our years that link has never been broken." **Oliver R Tambo**

"The transformation of our country requires the greatest possible cooperation between religious and political bodies, critically and wisely serving our people together. Neither political nor religious objectives can be achieved in isolation. They are held in a creative tension with common commitments. We are partners in the building of our society." **Nelson Mandela**

"The new South Africa born out of a broken and battered society, disfigured by the evil and corrupt apartheid system, cries out for hard political and socio-economic transformation which must be achieved if our country is to save itself from destruction. But it cries out also for spiritual power and resources to heal, to reconcile, to rebuild, and to restore its humanity. South Africa is crying out for its soul." **Thabo Mbeki**

As Jacques Delores looked for the "Soul of Europe," so Thabo Mbeki looks for the soul of South Africa and is determined to work towards bringing it to being.

The ANC know that learning about one another, understanding and respecting differences can only lead to a better society.

How many people in the UK have a good understanding of other cultures. I could have said other faiths, but the vast majority of British people have little or no understanding of the Christian faith, never mind Islam.

In the 2004 European Elections one of the Labour candidates on the list for the North West of England was Dr. Ebrahim Ayub Adia. He is a thirty something, university lecturer, married with two kids, a councillor on Bolton Council, speaks with a Lancashire accent, is a practising Muslim and is one of the nicest people you could wish to meet. Someday soon he will be a Member of Parliament and whoever he represents, they will get a good MP.

Ibby, like other Muslims I have known and spoken to about faith, is open and honest and it is always an education for me to have such a dialogue.

What follows is an account of a chat we had in June 2004, in the run up to the European Elections. His task had been a difficult one in trying to persuade the Muslim communities to keep their loyalties to the Labour Party following the war in Iraq.

"I do go to the mosque, but of course not anywhere near as often as I should go. I try to balance as best as possible the responsibilities that I have but I am often just overwhelmed with the workload. Balancing a full-time job, serving the local community as a local councillor and raising a young family is a challenge. It means that I cannot give the time that I should to my religion and that is a constant source of guilt. In Islam, one of the five principles, is the need to pray five times a day, and where possible to do that in congregation and preferably in a mosque. I find it almost impossible to get to the mosque during

126

the day but where possible I do catch a prayer in the office at work, or at home, on my own but this rarely amounts to five times a day.

I do really make a point of making it to Friday prayers in the mosque because it has to be part of congregation and of course during Ramadan I go out of my way to ensure that I take advantage of this special month."

I asked if he worked Fridays, to which he replied

"Yes I do work Fridays, but certainly I make a point to let...people know that it's very difficult for me to make the period between 12 o'clock and 2 o'clock in the afternoon. One example is that I've just become a non-executive director of the Primary Health Care Trust in Bolton. They sent me a series of dates on Fridays for an away day, and I said I have no problems with that, but I would have to be away during the lunch period for maybe an hour, so I do try and give myself enough space to catch Friday prayers."

Was he a practising Muslim, rather than a Muslim by...culture?

"I believe in all the fundamentals of Islam and I try to practise my religion as much as possible. As I have mentioned, Ramadan is one particular time where I really endeavour to practise my religion—so I wouldn't miss any of the fasts during the month of Ramadan and I would fulfil all my other obligations."

But as westernised as he is, I always think...it must be very difficult for first generation Muslim parents who come here to see their kids growing up in this society and becoming westernised. How does it affect them when they see their kids growing up not going to the Mosque?

"It varies...because of course first generation parents who came here were not all necessarily devout themselves,...so...what is fascinating is if you actually look at the social history of the first generation of Muslims...you have a...group of people who were concerned to preserve the faith, and they're the ones who were active in the community in establishing the mosque system for example.

"But then again there are other first generation parents who actually are not very devout themselves, and in some cases their children are more devout than they are."

When asked what percentage are devout, to give a ball park figure, he exhales and says

"I think that's an interesting one. I think if you probably asked somebody who was very devout, and again it's the definition of what devout means to different people...but I would say, if you took a definition of devout being people who attend five times a day for the Mosque prayers, or certainly managed to pray five times a day at home or at work, well I would say it was about 10/15 percent."

Which surprised me.

Ibby has a wonderful wife and kids so I asked him did he expect an arranged marriage?
"Yeah, well there was certainly an expectation that I would have an arranged marriage. My father...gave his father, who was on his death bed, an assurance that I would marry my first cousin in India, and therefore as I reached the age of...seventeen or eighteen I think, my relatives from India wrote and asked whether this arrangement could still go ahead. My parents asked the question and I said I didn't think it was what I wanted, and they wrote back and called it off. I was a little worried but my parents and for that matter my relatives in India were very understanding."

So how did this 34 year old Boltonian get into politics?
"I was sort of naturally inclined to politics, did GCSE Politics, then an A-level in Government and Politics, and then went on to do a degree in Public Administration. I had a natural interest in politics, and indeed I still recall from the age of 9 or 10, that I was very excited and looked forward to watching the 9 o'clock news with my father. So there was something in me from a very young age which attracted me to current affairs and the big picture. Active? I guess I became active as an undergraduate student, particularly as it coincided with the poll tax, all the student marches, but not active in any party political sense at the time. And I guess in many respects, in terms of an ideological...commitment I would say I was much...further to the left than I am now. I'm sure we've all been there! (laughs) Well, you get wiser as you get older! And more pragmatic and realistic! I then moved on to do a PhD, and...a few years after my return to Bolton, I think around 1997...I was fortunate enough to come across the Deputy Leader of Bolton Council, Guy Harkin. He asked me whether I would be prepared to do some part-time teaching at the University of Central Lancashire, in the area of Public Administration and I agreed.

"But he kept suggesting that I really should think about a political career, locally, to think about being a councillor, and he was very aware of the fact that Bolton, in spite of having a minority ethnic community of about 10%, had absolutely no representation on the council, all the 60 councillors were white, and had the usual profile of being aged as well. I held on for a few more years, just to make sure I established my academic career and then decided that I would take the plunge, and in May 2002 I decided to stand for the local council and was elected with a landslide.

"The year before...was my first real encounter with the Muslim community, because it was the general election, and the Labour MP, Brian Iddon was up for re-election. The Tories put forward a Muslim candidate and this caused a real dilemma in the Muslim community. For some Muslims it did not matter because they had voted Labour all their lives and were not prepared to change now. However, for others it did raise the question about loyalties and some people decided that having a Muslim MP, irrespective of the political party, was desirable. That proved a real personal struggle for me because I knew that a Tory MP representing a deprived constituency like Bolton South would prove disastrous and I decided to actively campaign with Brian in the Muslim community. Of course, some people suggested that I was disloyal and misinformed and that is difficult to listen to, not only for me but also for my family because we do live in the community. So the stance I take on issues affects not only me but also my family because my children attend a local school, they go to the local mosque, we attend weddings...so that's a constant issue for me, and to this day, as a local politician, that's something I have to keep in consideration.

"That was in 2001 and, and interestingly now, some of the very people who at the time were opposing Brian, now actually acknowledge that perhaps they weren't far-sighted enough. And if anything, they recognise that the Tory candidate had a limited understanding of politics, and probably would have done very little in Parliament to represent the interests of the Muslim community. And we've really been able to drive that home...with the local example, where we had a very long-serving Labour councillor in my ward, who had been the Chair of Planning, who had done excellent work for the Asian community, for the Muslim community in particular, but was still unseated in 2000 by a Tory...Muslim candidate. The Tory Councillor does not have any real connections with the local community, he does not live in the area, but at the time he was elected on the back of support from the Muslim community who felt that he would better represent its interests. People are now realising that he cannot deliver for the community. He's in opposition, there's nothing he can do, and there are some members of the Muslim community who are now arguing that it would have been far more desirable to have kept Jack. I think the two together have really created an awareness amongst Muslim voters in my ward that it's not necessarily in the best interest of the community to have a Muslim candidate but perhaps there needs to be a more sophisticated understanding of who is in power and what the different political parties represent."

So he was going to have to go through all of that again for the European elections because the Liberals had an Asian candidate
"Absolutely, he's Muslim, he's second on the Liberal Democrat list and he is promoting the idea to the Muslim community that...voting for him would give the Muslim community of Britain a voice in the European Parliament, and I'm sure that will appeal to a lot of people who feel that politicians have let the Muslim community down on the international stage.

"My role since 2002 has been very much to try and...engage with those who are seen as community leaders, mosque committee members and Imams, to try and help them understand the implications of the kind of direction they may give to the Muslim community. So I have argued on numerous occasions that support for individual candidates at election time should be based on a wider assessment of what different political parties stand for and this may mean that you end up voting against the Muslim candidate. This is the same argument I am taking to the Muslim community during these European elections but the Iraq conflict makes it a real challenge."

He joined the Labour Party when he was 16 years old, why?
"The youth worker at the local youth club, an Asian guy who had just graduated from Bradford University, really wanted to get some of us involved in local politics and he took us along to...several local Labour party meetings."

I wish there were more like him about!
"Interestingly several years later he stood as a Tory candidate, in the same ward, because he'd had enough of the Labour dominated Council, and the fact that the local Labour party seemed to be giving few opportunities to Asian candidates.

"So I went along to a few meetings, he gave us the application forms and said you really should think about joining. So I joined, but I wasn't in any way really active; I certainly didn't think about why I was joining the Labour Party in particular, at the time. But if you ask me that question now, I think certainly I'm much more clear as to why the Labour Party is still the right party for me.

Since the Iraq conflict, a lot of Muslims have abandoned the Party, but I am still arguing that the Labour Party is still the best party for the Muslim community. In terms of why Labour for me personally, I think that the Party's commitment to supporting the poor and vulnerable and its emphasis on social justice sits comfortably with my religious beliefs and that is a very important consideration because I believe that I will be held accountable for my actions after this life."

I raised the issue that when Tony Blair says that, he gets lambasted in the Press. 'I'll be held accountable for the Iraq war by my God,' or whatever he said, and he was lambasted for it. The irony is, Ibby can say it, but a Christian would be ridiculed in our society. If he and I were on a platform and he said that, no one would criticise him for it, whereas if I said it I would be seen as a nutter.

"I don't think it's seen as acceptable to bring religion into politics, particularly in a secular political system and this makes it very difficult for a Christian to make public statements. Perhaps a Muslim can get away with it because it is felt that Islam is a way of life and should inform all action and so politics cannot be an exception. Or perhaps, people are not willing to challenge a Muslim who makes statements about the way in which faith may influence his or her politics.

"Within Islam it's very clear that helping people, particularly the vulnerable and the poor, particularly... people who are in need, is very much rewarded and seen as desirable. In fact, it's seen as...something that every Muslim should think about and indeed one of the fundamental pillars of Islam is the principle of Zakaat, which is the two and a half percent wealth tax paid to the poor.

"I do find a lot of comfort in the fact that much of what the Labour Party stands for, in terms of redistribution of wealth...and...eradicating child poverty...trade union rights, workers' rights, all those types of projects which provide a safety net for people who are vulnerable...is something that I can live with, something I can promote, it's something that ...I feel totally comfortable with and totally committed to. So there's no significant conflict between what I believe in as an individual in terms of what my faith tells me...and what Labour Party policies are."

He's motivated by his faith and it's his faith that makes him do these things. Even if there was no Labour party he'd still want to do those things.

"Yeah, absolutely, it's fundamentally a preparation for the hereafter, and one way of making that preparation, to be held to account, is to be able to say, 'hang on, these are the things that I did in my short life' and it just so happens that I feel I can help people more if I am inside a political party rather than acting alone."

So if that applies to most Muslims why don't the most devout get more involved in party politics?
"Interestingly, it depends on how you understand your religion, and certainly for me, and the kind of things I draw on from my religion makes it possible for me to participate in politics. There are many others who might take a different interpretation and feel it almost impossible to participate in structures and institutions which operate on principles that are not Islamic. .

"And also, I think...one of the things you do have to be prepared for if you do get involved in politics is that you have to make compromises...you can't always peddle a particularly religious line. I think that would be very difficult for some Muslims to accept, I think they really would struggle with making those kind of compromises, for them it's a total belief system...and there are no compromises."

That's like saying, 'why isn't every Christian involved in politics?' It's the same type of thing. The Christian who's motivated by the same things that Ibby is doesn't often or always get involved. They do it through other things, they do it through the communities, they do it through the churches, they do it through their service, and the sacrifices that they make to...everyday people. That's how they do it.

And there are extremes in every religion. But how did he react, and how did his community react to the events after...or the events of September 11th, and...the suicide bombings, and the fact that after the Iraqi war now, we have that great dislike of the West, Blair in particular, and the Labour Party by...the Muslim community. Those guys who flew into the twin towers what would they say? Would they say they did it in the name of Islam? Or...what?
"I think...September the 11th has really put the...Muslim community in Britain in a predicament. Before September the 11th, I think there were people in Britain, Muslims, who felt confident that they could be British and at the same time preserve their faith. What's interesting here is, and I think

this is quite specific to Islam, is the notion of the Ummah, which is the international Muslim community, the world Muslim community. And the idea that stems from that, as a Muslim, it is your duty not only to worry about your Muslim brother who's your neighbour here, but to worry about all Muslims across the world, and the kind of reactions you therefore see in terms of...Iraq, or Afghanistan or Chechnya or Palestine really stems from that notion of looking after your brothers and sisters across the world...this means that Muslims are getting their loyalty questioned all the time. Are they loyal to Britain or do they have loyalties elsewhere? Since September the 11th I think the Muslim community feels under... immense pressure to integrate and to assimilate...and I think that's because there's been a change in the environment.

"There are some real hardline Islamic groups who I think are making life even more difficult for Muslims in Britain. Their views on establishing an Islamic state in Britain and support for the attack on the twin towers is treated by the media as if they are views held by the majority of British Muslims. Clearly, that isn't true and the majority of Muslims, and the Muslim Council of Britain, which gives leadership, were very quick to distance themselves from such thinking and to unequivocally condemn the attack on the twin towers. But there does remain a lot of bitterness about Palestine and Iraq and many Muslims in Britain feel that America is not even-handed in its dealings in the Middle East."

In this society in which you live, with pornography, booze, decadence...it's not what any parent want their kids to grow up in. So do Muslims see the West as being...a Godless place?
"Absolutely, I think fundamentally people are really concerned about the future of...the Muslim community in Britain...they are particularly interested in establishing institutions, in addition to the mosques...such as Islamic schools, to...ensure that the next generation of Muslims are strong in their faith, that they actually have a faith, and that they are not left vulnerable. It is very difficult...and that is a real concern."

As I look at our Asian communities in the UK and see their young people growing up I often feel it is a real threat to their community, as it has been with the Christian community which has taken a thumping since the war in this country. And I have visions of Islam going the same way, as you get generations who come along and start moving away from the faith.

Let's change the subject. Every time a suicide bomber...manages to do what they do in Israel...what's...the sort of reaction to that?

"It's not something that I ever discuss with people, it's not something that you sit down or happen to drop into a conversation. But I guess...by and large...the feeling amongst many British Muslims is that the Palestinians are dispossessed of their land...there's no clear future for their children, where...their women and children are humiliated at Israeli checkpoints...that kind of view does...hold very strong within the Muslim community. There are people not only in Britain, but around the world and of other faiths, who do feel that the Palestinians are totally helpless and have no other means left."

Does he profess his faith...publicly...or not?

"No, I don't profess my faith. Not publicly. No. I think some of my colleagues may actually impose that on me, and say it's part of my identity, and expect me therefore to support certain causes, but...I actually try very hard not to get...pigeonholed, because I actually think that makes it far more difficult to...represent the whole community.

"In actual fact, I'd say that the majority of my political colleagues would see me as...somebody who subscribes to social democratic values...and I think that helps me when it does come to promoting certain causes that the Muslim community want. Now what's interesting is there are other Muslim councillors, elected at the same time I was, and they have...very explicitly supported Muslim causes, and...perhaps indiscriminately...to the point where...I would argue that they are less effective in promoting the needs of the Muslim community, because they are seen as partial.

"I do choose my causes very carefully, and try to always consider the community cohesion dimension. I will support the Muslim community, but where it does not cause any wider damage because...ultimately, you know, there are occasions where there are people within the Muslim community who have a cause, but they don't see the wider implications. I think...in my case in particular there are my colleagues in the Labour group, and within the Party more broadly who judge me as someone who could be a potential parliamentary candidate, who could in future be representing Bolton South East or one of the Bolton constituencies, and therefore they need to see me as somebody who can represent the whole community, and that's not always clear for...people, for members of the Muslim community; they think I should be there advocating the kind of things they always want, and of course for me there are bigger issues of community cohesion that I have to think about.

"I can give you a couple of examples, one is that the Muslim community is pushing very hard for its own cemetery...the space they have at the moment will probably run out in two or three years in Bolton, and there's a clear view that Muslims ought to have their own area which they can manage themselves. Now...that's fine, it's a fair demand from the Muslim community, but, of course, the minute that's taken to the Labour group, or to the Council there are immediately people who ask, "Well why segregation even in death?" In addition there is the spectre of the BNP who would make political capital out of such a development so the issue has to be handled with great sensitivity and means that I have to tread a very careful path. So that's one type of issue.

"The other one where I did not support the community was where one mosque in my ward decided that they wanted to have the Azaam, you know, the call to prayer, they wanted to have that on the loudspeakers...in fact there was nothing in their planning permission to stop that. They came along and wanted to have a meeting with the Executive Member for the Environment, who was nervous about the possibility of this development. He asked for my view and I said "I don't think it's...a desirable development at this particular moment in time," because again I think it would get people's backs up in the area, non-Muslims and the BNP will cash in on it straight away. It's again, in the interests of community cohesion. And so he'd just asked me as a matter of fact, and the next thing he said was, "Will you come along to this meeting and say that?" I agreed to go along, I argued the case to the members of the mosque committee attending the meeting and they agreed. I think you do need to exercise leadership on such occasions and be prepared to take the consequences if there are any for the benefit of good community relations."

I think he's made the point that you don't have to shout it from the rooftops, you're driven by your faith, it's not about proclaiming your faith, it's being driven by it.
"It's about being driven by my faith rather than proclaiming it. It's about having a sense that you can provide a service to the community by being involved in politics and being clear that this commitment should extend to all communities that you represent and not only your own faith community.

"I've surprised council officers on a number of occasions, by stating that I believe that the Asian community in Bolton has had more than its fair share of resources in terms of housing regeneration for example, and I actually think that some of the white working class communities in council areas, but also in terms of private housing, have not had anywhere near the kind of investment that they deserve given the high levels of deprivation that they experience...So I've often argued that we must think very carefully about resources...and that as a matter of priority I think that resources should go into white working class communities...particularly if we're to deal with the threat of the BNP...and again, I've seen the surprise on the faces of...the head of the youth service when I said that I actually think that we really need to target white working class areas with...our youth work activities...and although we have a drugs problem within the Asian community, the problem's far greater within some of the white working class communities, and that the resources ought to be targeted there... Again there's an expectation sometimes amongst senior officers that I perhaps should represent a particular group of people, and it's interesting how surprised they are."

To conclude he said:

"It's a difficult subject really, because when we agreed to do this, I'd never sat down to actively think about the way in which religion...my religion and my beliefs influence the way I go about my politics...but clearly, my beliefs do influence the way I go about my politics, the decisions that I make and the battles that I decide to fight...indeed whenever I say a prayer...I always ask that I make the right decisions for the right reasons and to be free from corruption... Power has to be...exercised very responsibly, and I'm very clear about this, it's an immense responsibility and I will be held accountable."

Oh that more people could understand the likes of Ibby then barriers would indeed be broken down. But breaking them down is not always easy.

TEN

In the European Parliament there is an annual award called the Sakharov Prize, given to those who champion freedom of thought. It's been awarded to Nelson Mandela, Alexander Dubcek, Aung San Suu Kyi, amongst others. In 2001 it was given jointly to two people from both sides of the Israel / Palestinian divide who work to bring peace to their regions.

Izzat Ghazzawi was a member of the Executive Bureau of the Palestinian Council for Justice and Peace. He's been imprisoned and punished on a number of occasions by the Israeli authorities as a result of his political activities. His life was marked by the murder, by the Israeli army, of his 16-year-old son Ramy, killed in his schoolyard as he went to help a wounded friend. Despite this tragedy Izzat Ghazzawi continues to seek cultural and political dialogue with the Israeli people.

His co-award winner was Nurit Peled-Elhanan, an Israeli whose 13-year-old daughter, Smadar, was one of the victims of an attack carried out three years previously in West Jerusalem by a Palestinian suicide bomber.

"When my daughter was killed," Nurit said, "I did not give into despair and I made a speech which proved highly controversial, since it focused on the responsibility borne by those who implement a short-sighted policy which refuses to acknowledge the rights of others and foments hatred and conflict."

Nurit Peled-Elhanan has become the symbol of an Israel which is calling for a negotiated solution to the conflict and which clearly acknowledges the right of two peoples and two states to exist side by side on an equal footing. Through their lives and their commitment, Izzat Ghazzawi and Nurit Peled-Elhanan embody the hope of a negotiated, peaceful solution to the conflict between Palestinians and Israelis. Their personal tragedies have not turned them into enemies, their pain has not been transformed into hatred, but instead into the energy required to find ways of respecting the rights of individual citizens.

It was the 12 December 2001 when they came to the Parliament in Strasbourg to be honoured. Both spoke but the speech of Nurit Peled-Elham was so, so powerful. Here was the voice of a mother telling it like it is and in her wake brought many to tears. Eluned Morgan, a colleague of mine, who had recently given birth to her first baby was sobbing away as she listened in the original French that it was spoken in. Here is what she said:-

Madam President, ladies and gentlemen, Luisa, my family, Mrs Sartaoui, I wanted to dedicate this speech to the memory of my father and his Palestinian friend, Dr Issam Sartaoui, who both dreamt of peace thirty years ago.

I am, I feel, obliged, however, to dedicate this speech to the children who were killed yesterday by the Israeli army, simply because they were born Palestinians.

It is a great honour to be here today with you, as winner of the Sakharov Prize. I am well aware that, on such occasions, one should speak of hope and of the human qualities that can lead us to the triumph of compassion and fraternity between people. Forgive me, therefore, for not speaking of this today.

In Jerusalem, where I am from, hope and humanity are fading away. Israel is becoming a graveyard for children, which is growing bigger day by day. It is like an underground kingdom, extending beneath our feet and destroying everything in its wake. It is the kingdom where my daughter lives, with her Palestinian murderer, whose blood, mixed with hers, flows through Jerusalem, which became hardened to the sight of blood a long time ago. They are there with many, many more children, and they have all been let down. The murderer of my daughter has been let down, because his act of murder and of suicide achieved nothing. It did not put an end to the cruel Israeli occupation, it did not lead him to paradise, and those who promised him that his action would have meaning and value go on as if he had never existed. My young daughter was let down because she believed, just as thousands of her new brothers and sisters believed, that she lived in safety, that her parents protected her from evil and that nothing could happen to sweet little girls who cross the road to go to their dancing lesson. And all the children who are there with them have been let down, because the world goes on, as if their blood had never been spilled.

In Jerusalem, where I am from, the men who call themselves our leaders have allowed death to hold sway. It appears, however, that these gentlemen know how to live in peace when they have to. On Friday 1 December, the editorial of a local newspaper in a Jerusalem in mourning told us that there had been peace in Jericho for two months. There are no Israeli soldiers there, no Palestinian policemen, no gun shots.

Do not believe that the Americans have succeeded in convincing Ariel Sharon to stop sending young eighteen-year-old Israelis to kill innocent Palestinians, nor that they have succeeded in convincing the Palestinians to stop blowing themselves up along with their innocent Israeli victims. Far from it. Jericho is at peace because the Israeli and Palestinian leaders have together decided to reopen the casino …

When I read this article, I could not stop myself from thinking that my daughter's life is not even worth a single roulette chip. Almost 200 children have been killed since the beginning of the Intifada, of this incessant massacre, and they are worth nothing more than roulette chips. And yet, I was not very surprised, since I always knew that our war was not that of the Israeli people against the Palestinian people, but that of people who destroy lives who call themselves our Heads of State against the people from both sides.

These cunning politicians use God, the wealth of the nation, freedom and democracy, and even our periods of mourning as political tools, and they use our children as if they were figurines in their games of chance. For instance, you knock over ten of mine, and I shall knock over 300 of yours, and we will be quits until the next time.

None of this is new in the history of mankind. Leaders have always used God and other sacred values, such as honour and courage, to justify their self-indulgent ambition. And the only voice, throughout history, that spoke out to expose them and to oppose this was always the voice of mothers; the voice of those who produced the Jewish people, who disobeyed the Pharaoh's orders to kill little boys at birth; the voice of Rachel, our biblical mother, weeping for her children and refusing to be consoled; the voice of the women of Troy; the mothers of Argentina, the mothers of Ireland, Israel and Palestine. It is the voice of those who give life and who are committed to preserving it. It is the only voice that remains after the violence has subsided, and which truly understands the meaning of the end of everything.

Mothers are the only ones who know that the death of a child, any child, whether from Serbia or Albania, Iraq or Afghanistan, whether Jewish or Palestinian, is the death of the whole world, of its past and its future. When Luisa told me that I had been awarded the Sakharov Prize, I told her that I did not deserve it, since I had never saved a child, not even my own. But then I thought that the prize had not been awarded to me as a person, but to this voice that I took on through death and which transcends nationalities, religions, and even time. This voice that politicians and generals have tried to silence since man first walked this earth and since men have been waging war.

I have often been asked whether or not I feel the need to exact revenge for the murder of my daughter, who was only killed because she was born an Israeli, by a young man, who had so little hope that he was willing to kill himself and who only killed himself because he was Palestinian. I always quote the verse of the great Hebrew poet Bialik. 'Satan has not yet created those who would exact revenge for the death of a small child.' And this is not because Satan does not have the means, but because after a child has died, there is no longer vengeance, death, or life. The only feeling that remains, the only desire, the only need, that can never be satisfied, is that of protecting the child. The mothers who have lost their children will tell you that their arms hurt due to the constant need to hold the child and keep it from harm. No mother would ever think of seeking consolation by killing one child for another.

If we do not wish our entire planet to become a kingdom of dead children, we must raise our voices as mothers in order to silence all the other voices. We must once again listen to the voice of God who said 'Do not harm children.' Otherwise, there will soon be nothing

140

left to say, nothing left to hear, other than this incessant cry of mourning. Ladies and gentlemen, I beg you to listen to the voices that are coming from the underground kingdom of children who have been killed. That is where justice resides today, that is where true multi-culturalism holds sway, that is where we know that there is no difference between blood, between skin, between identity cards or flags. Listen to the cries of the dead children and help their mothers to save the children who are still alive.

The Official Journal then records that there was 'Loud and sustained applause.'

You can only appreciate these testimonies when you realize how big the divide is between the two communities. I've seen the same hatred in Kosovo and Bosnia/Herzogovina but I've also witnessed the Israeli/Palestinian divide at first hand. In 2003 running through to the early months of 2004 I co-chaired a Committee of Inquiry, in the European Parliament, into allegations of EU funds being used for terrorist purposes by the Palestinian Authority. We took evidence from a variety of people, visited the Middle East and heard "evidence" from both sides. What a place; what a problem; so much hatred that it seems to be irreconcilable.

So to hear Izzat Ghazzawi and Nurit Peled-Elhanan was refreshing and encouraging. This speech of hers truly was the voice of a prophet.

★   ★   ★   ★

Can prophets have no faith? I've described those who don't profess a faith yet fight for social justice, human rights, and freedoms as God's mercenaries or his Foreign Legion. If the world has to be changed and if we are God's hands to make those changes then God will wait a long time if he has to rely solely on those with faith.

So far everyone in this book has demonstrated how their faith motivates them, but how are the faithless motivated, what encourages them to do the good works that they do? To get some idea, I spoke to Louise Ellman, MP for Liverpool Riverside, and Glenys Kinnock, MEP for Wales.

I have known them both for a long time and have great respect for the work they have done as Labour politicians. Unfortunately my mini-disc with the interview with Louise was nicked from my Brussels office before it could be transcribed so this section is done from notes and not as comprehensive as I would have liked it to be.

Louise was the Leader of Lancashire County Council for many years until she went to the House of Commons in 1997. She comes from a traditional Manchester, Jewish, lower middle class background, whose grandparents were migrants from Russia, Poland and Lithuania.

Early on in our interview she made it clear she was a non–believer, her father had been an atheist and couldn't believe in a God after the holocaust. "Actually these days I say I'm agnostic; as I get older I'm less sure of things," she said. Yet, as she explained, she identifies herself as Jewish, eats Kosher food and does attend the major festivals at synagogue. In fact she identified with her Jewish ethnicity rather than the Jewish faith. Which is understandable, the state of Israel is full of secular Jews who, like Louise, have that same ethnic identity.

She said that when she was Leader of Lancashire County Council she could help solve problems that the Muslim population had, of which there are many in the Preston, Blackburn, Burnley industrial belt of the county, on issues such as Halal School meals and same-day burials and ensure these needs were met as she could identify with them.

Now her work with asylum seekers is motivated by her family's experience as immigrants and her late mother's friend who was a German refugee.

Her Manchester upbringing had with it the natural tendency to vote Labour, encouraged by her family and the Jewish youth groups (Habonim) she was involved with and so she began to take an interest in politics. So what was the motivation? "That feeling of wanting to right injustices for all, knowing what Jewish people had experienced," and the great Hebrew scripture tradition of making it a duty to care for 'Widows and orphans' as the prophets of old constantly reminded their people that someone had to care for the weak and vulnerable in society.

It's her Jewishness that makes her what she is, not necessarily (in fact certainly not) any faith in the God of her people.

Yet it is the teachings of the God of her people that were taught to her in her childhood and youth that make her the person she is today. Not unlike the other politician in this chapter.

If you were to ask the great British public to name an MEP, invariably they would say Glenys Kinnock. She's always had a high profile but there has always been more to her than simply being the wife of Neil Kinnock and her time as a Member of the European Parliament has shown this.

Her work on Development issues and fighting the causes of the Third World, especially Africa, is known far beyond the corridors of Brussels. She is hard working and dedicated to righting the wrongs of people in the Developing World. Being high profile does, however, have its drawbacks. She and Neil and her children get obnoxious treatment from some quarters of the British press, it's quite outrageous at times. I can always remember being on a delegation in Africa somewhere and Glenys couldn't dare sit by the pool to read her paperwork for fear of the papparatzi clicking their cameras to splash over the front pages of her being on a jaunt.

From 1989 to 1994 during my first term in the Parliament, I chose the Development Committee as my first choice but soon realised that I could do more for the causes of Third World development via the Budgets Committee. When Glenys was elected in 1994 it was good to have someone like her who knew the issues well. Up to that point I had been Mr Bananas, being an expert in the problems facing traditional Caribbean growers against the might of American multi-national companies. Glenys was quick to get involved and I eased out of Development to concentrate on Budgets. We did however go to the Windward Islands together in May 1997 on the very subject of bananas.

The interview I did with her only lasted thirty minute and on reflection, I wished it had been longer to pursue some of the issues she mentioned.

I had read Martin Westlake's biography of Neil and, towards the end when trying to assess what makes Neil the person he is, he writes:

"Kinnock, it should be noted is an intensely moral being. Jon Snow—a journalist who came to know Kinnock well has noted: 'He had a real conviction that came right from within' …….. Lord (Frank) Judd has observed; 'Neil is a values man. Although his honesty obliges him to maintain that he is an atheist, he belongs to the Christian Socialist tradition. His ethic is exactly that.'"

Westlake continues "Kinnock had indeed been deeply immersed in the Christian Socialist tradition; Mary Kinnock (his mother) was a devoutly religious person, and although Kinnock later lost his faith, he did not lose the values which had been so deeply inculcated in him."

So to begin the interview I said "I was interested when reading Neil's biography that both you and he came from non-conformist backgrounds, you were both Methodists, and you lost your faith during your university days?"

To which Glenys was quick to respond with, "Earlier for me, I am much more of a confirmed atheist than Neil is. Indeed in the current context in which religion is becoming more evident in politics as a result of Bush and religious fundamentalism it makes me more concerned about the need to confirm our secularism and the whole Charles and Camilla wedding there is the whole question of how much interference should there be by the Royal Family in religion and the fact that they are the head of the Church and what kind of an anomalous situation is that in the modern age."

She was keen to make the point and went at full speed. Alexander, an assistant who transcribed this text, said, "She has no full stops." She continued;

"I grew up in North Wales and my grandfather was a deacon. I used to help my grandmother cut up the bread for communion on a Saturday night. I liked the chapel because you had Sunday schools and outings. And then I was confirmed when I was about 14 and after that I never went to chapel again. After being confirmed I just felt this wasn't for me and completely rejected it. Although I carried on studying the Bible and religion in school, I got an A at A-level in Religion and that was because I found it very thought-provoking. I always liked the Old Testament stories and had a very good teacher in Religious Education who had a very wide-ranging knowledge of the issues which in those days was quite unusual. Whilst my family remained chapel goers and we got married in chapel, although we had to admit to the parson that we would be saying our vows with a certain amount of dishonesty, which he accepted, because it meant a lot to both of our parents. I am not sure I would do that now and I certainly did not want my kids to have religious weddings, which neither of them wanted."

So I asked "Why did it happen so suddenly, so soon after you were confirmed?"

"I don't know," was her reply. "I suppose because it is meant to be some kind of defining moment when you decide to become a full member of the Church. You accept what it says, and I just thought, 'What is all this gobbledy-gook? I don't want any of this. I don't think this is for me at all.' I talked to my dad about it. He would say, 'I am very sorry that you feel like that but as long as you have the values and the principles that go with it, which I think you do, then fair enough: that is your choice.'

"No one ever said that I was doing the wrong thing, or that I was disappointing them or anything of that kind. The British Labour Party has always been closer to Methodism than Marxism and that is really part of what I grew up with: the values of caring and the internationalism that went with it, talking about missionaries and starving African babies. That was the only place you heard about those things in those days. Combined with my dad, who had been in the Merchant service and travelled the world and had a great sense of what the injustices were. He always told me to fight against anyone who tried to oppress another. Even when I was about 15 I would join up with anti-Apartheid protests at the University in Bangor. Religion was part of my culture; it is what you take in with your mother's milk."

I asked, "What motivates you to do the things that you do?"

Her reply was absolutely clear, "I am not motivated by any religion, but I think I am motivated by similar values to what I would call good Christian values. My motivation is political. It is related to political solutions to the enormous problems we face."

I tried to find out what tells her what is right and wrong and she spoke about events in Africa, at which point I asked her why did she want to get involved in solving the problems of Africa. She replied:

"Well again it is political. If I have anything that motivates me, it is my socialist international approach that says that you can't close your own front door. That is why, in the Labour party, we say you can't opt out of wanting a good health service or education because you cannot disengage from what happens outside and the needs of other people because they are all directly related. September 11th has made that even clearer, that the roots of injustice and oppression are poverty. So whether it was my dad talking about his poverty in the 1930s when he couldn't get a ship and he spent time in Liverpool and Cardiff in seaman's hostels; a really disadvantaged upbringing: he left school at 14. That is a lot to do with why I feel such a need to tackle injustice. That does go back to the way my dad talked but also the same issues apply now, especially as we are so connected and we all want to get our kids into school, we want to get food on the table and we want a doctor down the road. Everyone wants that, it doesn't matter where you live. The accident of birth dictates that for many that does not happen and I am still seeing what I saw 20 years ago. I was just in Mozambique where I went with Neil when he was leader in the 80s and, although they are making enormous strides, it is like climbing up a sand hill. They are struggling, they have got nothing, no minerals or wealth of any kind. And yet there is a sense of purpose, of mission in that country but you just think: how can they keep on trying to make things better? They've had the war with the South Africans, involving themselves in all those front line states and still the struggle goes on. And now you see in Zimbabwe what a terrible tyrant can do to a country that shouldn't be a basket case, but is now because of oppression. So you just come round full circle all the time, but I am not pessimistic about our ability to do this. I am just doing a report for the Parliament on the Millennium Development Goals and I think they are achievable. Everyone says, "You can't do it, we won't do it for another hundred years," but we could now decide this year to put in place the means to do it. It is not beyond our wits to do it but always you come back to political will, whether there is the will to do that.

"Religion is creeping in, more and more unfortunately. For instance on the Millennium Development Goals, bringing down maternal mortality rates, thousands of women are dying. I was recently in Zambia a while ago. I met a man with four kids and he had tried to get his wife to a clinic when she was having a very difficult delivery and he had her in a wheelbarrow and she died in the wheelbarrow. I will never forget that."

"What has that got to do with religion?" I asked.

"Reproductive health rights," she said, "About saying these are the circumstances women find themselves in if they have too many pregnancies, they are not strong enough."

"You said that is where religion comes in."

"Because of Bush and the decisions that he took," she replied.

"But that tars everyone with the same brush," I said.

146

"It is becoming much more prevalent in this Parliament because of the new countries coming in with their own Catholic tradition." By this she was referring to the ten new Member States of the EU, especially a country like Poland. "Increasingly you cannot talk rationally about these things because you are seen as an extremist who wants to offer abortions left, right and centre which is not the case at all.

"I do not believe that God decides who should live or die, but this is what we are beginning to hear from fundamentalists on all sides whether they be Christians or whatever. I fear this change that I feel is taking place, this new acceptance of a view which obviously went down a bomb in America. We thought they were queuing up to vote for Kerry but they were queuing up to vote for the religious right that Bush represented. I am very unnerved by this."

"Do you class anybody of faith in that category?" I had to ask.

"No, absolutely not. I know how much deep concern there is."

When asked, what about the fact that she must have had to work with churches in a variety of African countries, she was clear:

"Who is the one speaking out in Zimbabwe? Archbishop Pius in Bulawayo. He is amazing. I have met him a number of times and he is a wonderful guy. He has the guts to preach every Sunday about the truth. Tutu in South Africa; if in the Apartheid days we hadn't been able to work with the churches then we would have had nobody to work with."

So isn't it a problem that those type of people will get condemned because of fundamentalists?

"Often they can be disappointing. Rowan Williams disappointed me massively by giving in to the pressure he was under. I have known him for a long, long time in Wales and I don't believe he believes that. I think he has made an enormous mistake."

Where did he come into it, I wondered, on the issue of gay priests?

"And on abortion," she said. "He could have said it is not necessary for us to look at this issue. Let's get on with other things. But he just followed the lead of others, which I found disappointing. That is the danger, that it becomes a consensus amongst those who have different faiths, that this is what your constituency expects of you and there is a manipulation of these issues by fundamentalists of various kinds."

This is a long way from Tony Hall's interview.

Glenys went on, "One of the things we would say is that a woman has a right to have access to a safe abortion, if the baby is going to die or she has had too many pregnancies, then Marie Stopes will give abortions. Otherwise you get Vera Drake stories. But they have withdrawn all funding from any organisation that gives any abortions. You can't do that in poor countries. They haven't got access to contraceptives. If you meet a little girl of 12 in the Congo who has been raped and she is having a baby, these people would say, 'Yes she must have it.' Well I wouldn't say that, because what hope is there for either of them? Or if you meet a woman who knows she is HIV positive and says, 'I don't want this baby because it will be born HIV positive and I will die before it is able to look after itself.' My sympathy is with her.

"There is a paragraph in my report, which is very measured. The right in the Parliament will vote against it. In the past it would have got through but not in this Parliament."

I mentioned my visit to South Africa, when I visited Winterveldt. At a Catholic-run clinic, they were dishing out contraceptives and said they saw it as protection, not contraception, which I thought was a wonderful phrase.

"They do this because they live in the real world," she said. "Last time I was in Zimbabwe I visited a Catholic nursery looking after orphaned kids and they were going round, all day, giving food to dying AIDS people and they see the effects of neglecting these people. AIDS now is a women's disease and until women can have some control themselves without their husbands even knowing, because that is the major problem, that men can't be persuaded to use them."

I knew we were time limited so I changed the subject and mentioned that I heard her on a faith programme on Radio 2 a couple of years ago and was surprised she was on it. "Why do you do those kinds of programmes?" I asked.

"It is important that we all talk to each other. I don't hate religion and I really respect so many people who have done so much. That programme reflects the real interest which the church has in overseas issues and has always had.

"I think you are either someone who needs to have that comfort or not. I just don't feel I do. I just don't feel I need to think that there is something going on there or somebody looking after me. I think there is the forces of good and the forces of evil and I think you have to overcome the forces of evil and you do that in whatever way you can.

"In many ways people like yourself share many similar values, and Labour Party allegiances, as I do, you just happen to go to church on Sunday and I don't."

It was at this point where I should have asked her to elaborate. Shouldn't I have pursued the forces of good and forces of evil remark? Of course I should, but I didn't.

I did make the point that having a faith is not simply about going to church. I should have also said it's not about having a comfort zone but she was too quick for me.

"A lot of people say they feel envious of those who have the comfort that religion can give you and I think that it must be the case. I am not envious at al. That is not because I have some inner strength that others do not, but I have rejected it more and more as time has gone on. I think Neil has more and more as well."

I remembered Louise Ellman's comment about being less sure the older she gets. Was Glenys the same?

"That is not the case with me. I am more and more entrenched in the view I have."

Okay then the question to ask any atheist, "How do you express thanks? For example when your kids were born?"

She leaned back and laughingly said, "I thanked God the bloody thing was over with." Said as a simple comment not as a religious statement.

"I don't give thanks, to be loved and to have love, which I have been very fortunate to have. A very happy upbringing and wonderful family, I am very close to my kids, good friends with them. I get comfort from that and their love but it is a question I can't answer, because I don't feel the need to thank. I don't think any of these things happen without efforts. You don't have a happy family life unless you have invested a lot in it, it doesn't happen by default. It happens because you've been good parents and you've cared about your kids. It is also about what you bring with you into a marriage and a family. I suppose I thank where I come from more than anything else."

"Have you ever discussed this with the likes of Tutu?" I thought and asked.

"No," she responded. "People don't talk about religion very much any more. Do they?"

"I do."

"My close friends never do. I think it used to be what people talked about. If you read 19th Century novels you realise that religion was a vein running through everything, which it isn't any more. I suppose that is why there is a bit of a rear-guard action to try to bring people back to that affiliation which doesn't exist anymore. I don't think people feel that need so much now to have a faith. People are nervous about not saying they are Christians but they don't go to church."

I tried to make the point that it's not that people don't believe in something, they tend to believe in anything these days, whether it is new age or whatever. At which point she assumed that a lot of young people have no faith to which I made the point that many young people are actively involved in churches.

Surprisingly she said, "Don't they sort of 'see the light'—there is quite a lot of that going on, an evangelical approach. Sometimes if I catch 'Songs of Praise' and see the wild way in which people behave, I think 'God, this is embarrassing for me to look at, what is going on in their heads?' They get going on this massive happy-clapping event. They are obviously very happy though."

I commented that in Australia the Anglican Church is booming because it is evangelical. They have very young congregations and it is the evangelical churches that are growing.

Glenys tends to have very clear cut views and said, "That is because of all the razzmatazz that goes with it. We were talking about Africa; I think there is a resurgence of religion in Africa both Christian and Muslim. You can see that in the tensions that are developing and the churches becoming more and more influential and powerful. You see Afro-Caribbean communities in the UK all going to church because it is part of their community. And also you can have a good time. If your life is terrible then to put your best on on a Sunday and go and have a good sing, I can't think of anything better. We go to the Millennium Stadium to do that.

"I know Bible stories and songs, I know them all, and Neil does. He will always quote verses of the Bible in speeches and so on. I never do. It is always there. I think my kids have a huge gap in their education really, they don't know about all that. There has been a lot written recently reassessing St Paul, whether he was a spin doctor, but if you read Paul it is wonderful, sheer poetry, at least in the King James' version, as history and stories.

"As history and stories.... I do believe that Jesus lived and was one of the greatest people who ever lived. He demonstrated an amazing ability to grasp both political situations and be compassionate and brave. He was a hero and the Bible is full of heroes. It is a terrible gap in the current generation's knowledge that they don't have that."

"Are you a militant atheist?" I asked already knowing the answer.

"Yeah, religion really, really gets to me. I am not ambivalent, I am absolutely clear on my views and I know they won't change. I don't think any circumstances will make me believe."

If Louise or Glenys (or Neil even) had been in the audience when Jim Wallis asked, "Where are the prophets?" they would have been up on their feet shouting, "We're here," along with the rest of them. It's clear to see the roots of their motivation but it also indicates something else. Doing good works is not necessarily done to glorify God or his creation. On the other hand, believing in God should be expressed by doing such good works, but it is more, much more than that. It comes back to that thing about a relationship with God.

Brussels can have some dark, damp winter mornings. The type of days when the rain feels like it can penetrate any waterproof that you challenge it with.

On one such morning, several years ago, I'd caught the tram from my flat just after 7.30am, changed at Montgomery to take the Metro to Maalbeek and then walked to Parliament. This was not my usual routine; normally I would take a car and be dry all the way, so when I exited Maalbeek metro station onto Rue de la Loi I had to decide which was the best way to go to get least drenched.

But wet, wet, wet I was, as I turned off Rue Belliard; I realized that there must be a rear route into the Parliament through the garage which would save me walking a few more hundred metres in the rain to the main entrance. But which way to go, how to do it?

There in front of me was my pathfinder: a twenty-something young woman, about to use the 'tradesman's entrance'. The cleaners would already be at work so she probably worked in the catering department—most of them arrived just before 8am. Ten metres in front of me she turned into the garage area, so did I. Fifty metres further she went through security and said 'Bonjour' to the guys operating the scanning machines; five seconds later so did I. She opened a door and went up two flights of steps, so did I. She opened another door into a corridor and I followed close behind; only the two of us about. She went into another door and as I followed she turned in shock and, in French, in effect said, "What the hell are you doing?" Equally shocked my eyes looked at the outline of a female on the door and realized I had entered a ladies toilet. In spluttering, broken French, I try to say "sorry...ooops," "wrong door," back off and find the right turn to get me into the body of the Parliament, hoping I would never see her again in my life. I had visions of her being in the canteen and pointing me out, "There he is. There is the pervert."

The moral of the story? It helps if you have an idea of where you are going and following the wrong person can terminate in an unexpected ending. During a discussion in Strasbourg at one of our monthly Prayer Breakfasts I made a comment about having a faith being an integral part of one's life. I'd said something about how faith can enrich life. "Don't assume that faith always refers to religion," said one of my colleagues. "Faith itself is not necessarily something positive. My father had a faith in Communism and I too shared that faith for quite some time."

Jürgen Schröder is a Christian Democrat MEP from East Germany and he'd suddenly made me want to explore further. Some time later I had the chance to sit down and talk to him about this. He explained his comment above saying, "We should know what we are believing in. People can believe and have faith in superstitions or idols." So what had he and his father believed in?

Jürgen was born in 1940 and didn't really see his father until he returned after the war to their home in Saxony-Anhalt. This non-Christian bank clerk had been conscripted into the army and had been a prisoner of war of the Americans, held in France until his release in 1947. In East Germany at that time the Social Democrats and the Communist Parties had a forced marriage to form the Socialist Unity Party, the SED. And it was to the SED that he went when he came home. "Given a choice he would possibly have been a Social Democrat, but there was no choice," said Jürgen, "He never spoke of the war, he hated it, but said that he joined the SED to prevent any future wars."

During his father's absence his mother had said they should pray for his father's return home and so at the age of six his mother had taught him how to pray. "I remember being in the village church on Christmas Eve in 1946 and having a really good feeling of being there," he said.

The following year he started school and like most other kids in the village he also attended a religious class once or twice a week outside of school hours. "One time I told Dad that the teacher had been speaking about the Devil and that it had scared me," he recalled, "So Dad went to see the teacher and told him I wouldn't be attending any more."

Somewhere around fourteen or fifteen years of age he became a Marxist after reading the East German philosopher, Georg Klaus, who had written a book on "Jesuits, God, Matter", where he countered the version of Christianity put forward by a West German Cardinal. It was convincing enough for him to know that he wanted to be a Marxist.

For his higher education he went to East Berlin in 1960 to study Philosophy. Loaded with plenty of philosophical questions he found that he wasn't getting answers from the professors; they were after all Party liners. "One of them, Kurt Hager, lectured on Das Kapital and was boring and didn't even touch on what 'man' was about. There was no-one to discuss the type of things I wanted to talk about. Marxism was all about historical materialism where man played no role. Individuals only had to fulfil the historical laws of materialism, which gradually I began not to accept," said Jürgen.

"We were allowed to read German classical philosophers and in some of these

I found other approaches. Reading Emmanuel Kant and other such philosophers opened my eyes in so far as he did not put Mind and Matter as opposites." Jürgen then explained how in Marxist teaching these two were opposites and he found that hard to accept, so he then stopped studying philosophy because he feared if he were to continue it would prevent him being a Marxist. "The aim of such study was to produce a Marxist and I felt that I might become someone else and that would have been more dangerous for me than to quit. To give answers in my examination that were not in line with the official ones would have been a greater crime."

He was then sent to work in a factory and did so to illustrate that he wasn't an enemy of the State. He stayed there for two years and during this time, with the help of an old teacher, taught himself English (he had already done Russian, French and Latin at school). "In a mundane routine job it was easy to concentrate on what I was studying." From the factory he went back to studying, this time English and French, to graduate as an interpreter and translator in these two languages.

During this second time of studying he rediscovered his liking for philosophy and, when asked by fellow students, he joined the SED. He had become a card carrying Communist. "But I was unhappy right from the start, I'd actually believed that you could change things from the inside but soon realized I couldn't. You either go with the herd or you are isolated. I carried on reading literature that criticised the system. I also had a lot from the Austrian Communist Party, which was highly critical of the Soviet Communist Party, as was the Italian Communist Party. Here was dissident behaviour in the Communist world. Events in Czechoslovakia I followed with interest and before the 'Prague Spring' came to an end in August 1968 I applied to leave the SED and was subsequently chucked out in May of that year after four years of membership. I no longer believed in Marxism, that is I was no longer a materialist and the SED were against the aspirations of decent people in the Soviet bloc particularly in Czechoslovakia."

"This was a really hard decision. Interestingly my interrogators were not interested in my motives but in *who* had influenced me. If any of my work colleagues showed any sympathy for me they would be punished. I told them they had to disown me. Upon leaving the Communist party and returning my party card and booklet I had to go through something akin to a religious rite. Communism was a system that subjugates people and it needed rites and symbols. It wasn't easy and it was indeed a problem for me, I was constantly asked why did I leave the Party? My father felt offended and my mother being the loyal wife that she was supported him in his feelings. I hadn't given them any indication that I was even thinking of leaving so that when they were challenged by the authorities they could honestly deny any knowledge of it. Mum was very subservient of Dad yet I know that clandestinely she still paid the church tax."

He went on to describe the relationship that thereafter existed between his father and him. As an 18-year-old he went with his father to take their names off the Church membership role (everyone in Germany was on one). Now a frosty relationship existed to such an extent that they simply agreed never to discuss politics.

As for becoming a Christian, well he certainly wasn't when he left the Communist party and wasn't for many years to come. However, "It was the interplay of various factors from people I knew, or met, and things I read," that led over a number of years to him becoming a member of the Lutheran Church in 1978.

"I was always trying to find something to fill my soul; there were positive co-incidences which kept playing a part in my development. From the six-year-old who had been taught to pray (incidentally I had been baptised as a baby) to the lack of answers at university. I had bought a Zurich Bible as part of my philosophy studies and began to read it. How boring. It's difficult to become a Christian when you have to read lots of begetting. I put it to one side.

"After I left the Party there was a vacuum and thankfully it wasn't filled instantaneously. Christianity didn't come along and catch me on the rebound. It was a real gradual process, discussing with colleagues and friends, reading a lot. I read a lot in English. The English language helped to form my way of thinking, I learned a lot about democracy and religious things. Learning English really changed my outlook, although it was American rather than British stuff that I was reading. A British mechanic who was in Leipzig to repair a machine gave me 'Future Shock" by Alvin Toffler, an American, which was published in 1970 and spoke about adapting to change; this helped me a lot. Another co-incidence or God-incidence."

"Inside of me something was growing until, at the age of 38 or 39, I began attending Church on a regular basis. When I am asked about what is the most important thing to me I answer 'my faith'. I pray that I may never lose my faith otherwise I would go mad."

He joined the East German Christian Democrat Union (CDU) in 1979 which to the West was seen as a puppet of the system. It certainly wasn't a sister party to the West German CDU, on the contrary. He tells how he joined for two reasons: first to feel protected in that no-one from the Communist party would then reproach him, and second to contribute to society. The CDU did lots of voluntary community work, looking after parks or streets or embellishing villages. Also the CDU owned a daily newspaper where you could learn about religious matters and they also "had a broad gamut of educating people which was not possible in the USSR or Czechoslovakia."

"The CDU was a haven for those who left the Party and you could deal with religious issues. I'll tell you, in the old East German CDU we talked more about God than we do in the modern day CDU, probably because we had no power but more time."

As East Germany went through its upheaval, he stood for the first democratically elected Parliament. "The rank and file asked me to stand but my wife didn't like the idea." He entered the Volkskammer with the CDU as the largest party going in coalition with the Social Democrats. "The CDU may have been the largest party but people didn't vote for the 'C' (i.e. Christian), they voted D for the Deutschmark. I became European Affairs Spokesman for the CDU and in February 1991, I became one of the East German Observers to the European Parliament and have subsequently been elected and re-elected in 1994, 1999 and 2004.

"In the end my mother was happy that my career had a path to it when she saw me get elected. As for Dad he developed Alzheimer's disease and when the SED became the PDS he asked me to help him resign, not for ideological reasons but because of their behaviour." I remembered the film 'Goodbye Lenin,' a story of East Germany's change to capitalism, and mentioned it. "It was not unlike that," he said.

That chance comment of his in Strasbourg at the Prayer Breakfast that "Faith in itself is not necessarily something positive" and "Don't assume that faith always refers to religion" led me to discover this fascinating story of a man who finally arranged to follow the right person.

At another of the Strasbourg Prayer Breakfasts just after the death of Pope John Paul II, Claude Moraes MEP, one of my British colleagues (let me explain his parents are Indian and came from Goa, he was brought up in Scotland and has a Scots accent, and represents London, not your normal MEP, Oh and he's a Roman Catholic) was leading the discussion. He mentioned how several of his Aunts were nuns in India and did some tremendous work amongst the poor. As a nine-year-old he asked one of them, who was visiting Scotland, why she prayed so much and why wasn't she spending that time doing good. The discussion then got round to the importance of prayer and at that point Tunne Kelam from Estonia made a wonderful intervention.

"When you live in a totalitarian regime, where the State can do anything to you and controls everything," he said, "The only things you have left is prayer and hope. And prayer can be so powerful at changing things."

Which reminded me of what he had said in his interview and what Ulrich Meisel and Maat Laar had said. This is not a comfort zone they are talking about, but an absolute assurance zone. That is also why Jürgen treasures his faith.

He has the ability to say the right thing at the right time. On another occasion the piece of scripture being discussed was the one about "being salt of the earth." Tunne intervened to say, "It's not that there is too little salt but there is too much sugar. Everyone these days wants La Dolce Vita."

In both cases, Louise and Glenys show how the faith of their families, their cultures, affected their political views. But what of future generations, fewer people of faith, a more secular society, fewer people interested in politics, how are the young to get their motivations?

Is our affluent society to be one of individualism, that is with no Ubuntu, kids living for binge boozing and a drug culture? Well it doesn't have to be. Many young people do want to get involved. In the UK the big fund-raising telethons such as Red Nose Day or Children in Need invariably get schools raising lots of money. Live Aid and Live 8 concerts help to raise awareness but once the hype has faded, once the music has finished, what are the donors doing then?

Giving to charity may salve our conscience for a while but it isn't giving the Soul that is needed in society.

Doing good works is not the monopoly of believers, but to do good works, to set people free from tyranny, from hunger, from want, you have to have a driving force to do it, especially when you are on the receiving end of the oppression.

ELEVEN

In the early nineties my Brussels office had a call from a British Fire Authority asking if we could help. At that time there was a European Directive going through the decision-making channels about hazardous chemicals. On the rear of every petrol tanker, chemical tanker or whatever is transporting hazardous material is a plaque with a code on it. This is there so that in the event of an accident the fire fighters know how to treat any spillage. These codes come under the Hazchem regulations or something like that.

Anyway, the EU was trying to standardise the codes for the twelve member countries at that time and apparently there was a problem with the Danes. So the request from the British was, would we organize a meeting of Danish MEPs so that they could give a presentation to them. No problem, we'll make some enquiries, get on with it, Maire (my then assistant—pronounced Moira as in Irish).

Unfortunately the next phone call from them, a day or so later, said something like, "Oh, by the way, we will be in Parliament at 3.00.pm. on the 6th May, or whatever it was but it was precise and the flight and hotels had been booked. Maire, this is all yours. I'm leaving it to you. In true Pontius Pilate fashion I washed my hands of it.

Now bear in mind, this is before the days of mobile phones or e-mails, to have a fax was a luxury. Also there were only sixteen Danish members and there was no guarantee that any of them would be there at that time and date. Maire telephoned, faxed and went to their offices for days and days but with little success. Trying to get politicians to commit to anything at the best of times is always a problem so her task was doubly difficult. But she tried and tried as resolutely as she could.

Come the day she hasn't got any Danish MEPs. A call comes to the office from reception, there are some visitors that need signing in. She duly signs them in and takes them to my colleague Brian Simpson's office.

"If you'd just like to wait here, gentlemen, I'll go and get the Danish MEPs into the meeting room, then I'll take you there," she said.

As she came out of Brian's office who did she see but David, a twenty something assistant strolling down the corridor with a swagger of confidence that his generation have.

"David, David," she said, rushing up to him and quickly explaining the situation. "I want you to be a Danish MEP, I'll get three or four other assistants, go to the room, listen to what they have to say, nod your head a few times, don't speak, shake their hands, then leave."

"No problem, Maire, lead on," was his response.

Full of pride at her brilliant idea, she set off down the corridor with David in tow. The worst thing she could have done and did, was to stop at Brian's office. She popped her head in the door to announce, "I have one of the Danish members here, we are just going to the meeting room." At which point David brushes her to one side and makes an entrance into the office with the words, "Hello, my name is Sven" in the phoniest Danish accent you can imagine. Maire's jaw dropped then mouthed silently, "N-o-o-o-o, David, N-o-o-o-o."

Sounding like the Swedish chef out of the Muppet Show he continued, "I tink I am de only Danish member here today. You come and give me your pres-en-ta-tion and I will pass on all you say to my colleagues." After shaking their hands furiously he led them out of the office towards the elevators with Maire smiling sheepishly trying to conceal her horror.

In the lift he is giving it plenty, "Vat a bu-ti-ful day it is, is it not," until one of these fire officers begins speaking in Danish. Now this has to be the only Danish-speaking fireman in the UK. Quick as a flash David responds with "Do you mind if we speak English, I'm trying to practise my English."

"But you have a northern accent," says the fireman.

"I've spent a lot of time in Viggan" David replies. The lift is going from the third floor to the ground floor, when it stops at the first floor.

The doors open and stood there is Mel Read, a British Labour MEP. "Hello, David, how are you?" she says, to which he steps out of the lift, takes her by the arm and marches her off down the corridor saying "Very well, Mel, but keep walking."

Poor Maire's left in the lift as the doors close, has to apologise for this typical Danish behaviour. "Funny buggers, these Danes" was the final sentiment of the firemen.

A true story with a moral; don't pretend to be someone you are not.

So how should a Christian in politics behave and is there any pretence about the role?

There's an old saying that nothing is politically right that is morally wrong. But Christians will have a variety of views on issues like abortion, homosexuality, the war in Iraq, or wars in general. Christians come from all sides of the political spectrum, this book illustrates that, my Baltic and Balkan examples are of the centre right, not all would associate themselves with Cedric Mayson's socialist position, not even many in New Labour. In other words the definition of a moral wrong could differ from person to person.

I've taken decisions or done things that have had the response, "I thought you as a Christian would have done the opposite," said by Christians and atheists alike. Politicians live in a secular world and have to make difficult decisions all the time. Was Tony Blair, as a Christian, wrong to go to war in Iraq? Whatever your answer, in that circumstance he is not just a Christian but a Prime Minister faced with a variety of decisions. In fact, he did say in one interview he would be judged by God (which led to a lot of ridicule).

In the British Labour Party, as in all political parties, there are many people with great ideals who always criticise their governments, when in power, for some of the decisions they have to take. It has always been so.

But idealism may never actually achieve anything. Politics is about achieving what is possible, which often means compromising, sometimes compromising on things you feel strongly about.

In the UK where there is first-past-the-post politics, when the politician votes it's either a win or lose situation. If you have the majority you will invariably win and if you are in the minority, well tough. In the European Parliament no political group has a majority and to get legislation through the Parliament requires a qualified majority of 50% plus one of the MEPs. Note, it's not 50% of those voting plus one, but 50% of the 732 actual members. So the magic figure of 367 votes in favour is needed to get legislation through. This means compromises have to be reached. The largest political group, at the time of writing, is the People's Party of Europe (PPE) the centre-right grouping with 267 members, followed by the Party of European Socialists with 201, neither of which can succeed without getting the support of other groups or working together.

That has meant learning to compromise, which is not normally the way that British politics works, but it does get results and you can get the achievements you seek.

In all three of my offices I have pinned up on my wall a text of what Dennis Healey said at the 1959 Labour Party Conference. He refers to it in his book *The Time of my Life* and this is what he writes:

> *"I myself went to Blackpool with no intention of speaking, since there was to be no debate on foreign policy—the only subject on which I had ever addressed our Conference till then. The frightening refusal of so many delegates to face the reality of our defeat finally forced me to my feet.*

> *"I pointed to the growing gap between the Labour activists and the voter.*

> *"Hugh Gaitskell was absolutely right when he said yesterday that what gets cheers at this Conference does not necessarily get votes at elections. If it did we would have won Devonport (the seat which Michael Foot had just lost). There are far too many people who .... want to luxuriate complacently in moral righteousness in Opposition. But who is going to pay the price for their complacency?*

> *"You can take the view that it is better to give up half a loaf if you cannot get the whole loaf, but the point is that it is not we who are giving up the half loaf. In Britain it is the unemployed and old age pensioners, and outside Britain there are millions of people in Asia and Africa who desperately need a Labour Government in this country to help them. If you take the view that it's all right to stay in Opposition so long as your Socialist heart is pure, you will be 'all right, Jack'. You will have your TV set, your motor car and your*

summer holidays on the Continent and still keep your Socialist soul intact.
The people who pay the price for your sense of moral satisfaction are the
Africans, millions of them, being slowly forced into racial slavery; the Indians
and the Indonesians dying of starvation.

"We are not just a debating society. We are not just a Socialist Sunday
School. We are a great movement that wants to help real people living on this
earth at the present time. We shall never be able to help them unless we get
power. We shall never get power unless we close the gap between our active
workers and the average voter in the country.

"Thirty years later I am still making the same speech."

He reflects my point of view wonderfully well. There is little point being in
politics unless you can influence decisions and change those things you want to
change. To be a backbench opposition member in the House of Commons
must be extremely frustrating. At least in the European Parliament every
individual member has the possibility to influence legislation and to get things
done.

Fundamentalists, of whatever persuasion, religious or not, are fortunate in that
they know what is absolutely right. THEY are absolutely right. For mere
mortals like me the world is not in black and white but has a lot of grey areas.

Not only are there grey areas but the politician could well have split loyalties.
In the case of Labour MEPs first there is the loyalty to your constituents, the
people who elected you; but the problems of rural Cumbria are not the same
as urban Manchester or Liverpool and therefore your constituents' needs will
differ. Then there is the loyalty to your party and party workers who not only
put you up as a candidate but did the hard graft needed to get you elected.

For Labour members the Trade Unions will also expect loyalty to help get
legislation that benefits their members. This does not always match the needs
of the UK Government as shown when the Working Time Directive had to
be voted upon. The Unions lobbied in a contradictory manner to the Labour
Government. Of course, you can't ignore the interest of UK plc and that
becomes another influence. And for the Christian, Muslim or Jew there are
other factors. (At this point I'm reminded of Ulrich Miesel and "only God is
almighty." Well then, help me balance these loyalties, God, and I have to hope
to take the right decisions.)

Glenys Kinnock is very committed to fighting the wrongs of the Third World and knows what is right and what is wrong when it comes to alleviating poverty or giving the least developed countries a fair deal, and that, of course, is another influence and loyalty.

When she and I returned from our visit from the Windward Islands, looking at the problems of the Caribbean banana producers, we went to see Sir Leon Brittan, the then European Commissioner for Trade.

The problem was one of small Windward Islands producers trying to compete against American multi-nationals with huge plantations in Central America. World trade being governed by the WTO meant that these traditional producers who had been used to guaranteed market access and good prices in Europe were under threat from the bigger producers. The EU had done a lot for them but there were limits to what could be done because of the WTO.

We explained the situation, of which he was aware of course, and then he explained why, because of WTO rules, things were developing the way they were. It was a good explanation and I understood well his reasoning. Not Glenys, it was wrong, pure and simple. So he explained again, it made no difference, it was not fair on these countries and she was right but there was little that could be done. He tried a third time but she would not be convinced. She knew what was right and what was wrong about the WTO rules.

Like many constituents who come to me when the courts have ruled against them and they say, "It's not fair." I have to tell them that the bells of law and justice seldom ring together. That's what you have to realise and accept in the world of politics, you can't solve everyone's problems and what is seen as the law in this world is not always just.

So does that make Glenys, the atheist, a prophet and me, the Christian, someone pretending to be one? Why compromise on an issue such as this, when it is clearly a moral wrong? Is trying to work with the European Commission to alleviate the effects of the WTO rules rather than demanding the rules be changed really the course to take?

You may not be able to solve everyone's problems but you can fight for them and that means trying to convince others that things have to change. That takes time and effort (ask Tunne Kelam et al.) and facing up to frustrations but it has to be done.

The banana issue is still with us and Glenys is still leading the fight. It comes back to giving Europe a soul, because this particular fight is against big, multi-national companies with plenty of clout. The EU should not be merely an economic entity but should have (and does have to some extent) the ability to look beyond economic needs to help those the prophets cry out for.

I don't intend repeating the discourse on contentious issues, such as homosexuality and abortion, which are covered at length in my previous book, except to say that not all people of faith have the same opinions on these and other issues such as war, gambling, prostitution, the death penalty, immigration and probably every other issue that has political connotations. In other words, there is no off-the-shelf version of the Christian politician.

I'm sure some people feel that those politicians who profess a faith are a soft-touch on certain issues (I don't think Ian Paisley or John Ashcroft would agree, or even those from those countries who had totalitarian regimes). Why this is, I am often left wondering, as I said in an earlier chapter, Jesus was a tough, revolutionary prepared to take on the authorities, he was no soft-touch so why should his followers be seen to be so?

He preached a message of loving God and loving your neighbour as yourself, these were his two great commandments. Do these things and all else follows. What matters is how you live your life trying to fulfil these two instructions, how you reflect His commandments to others. It matters how you do this in life in general but in politics in particular and the type of person you are matters; the perception that others have of you by professing your own faith in your political life is probably also the perception that they have of your worshipping faith, whatever it may be.

Some of the people I have know in my political life, like in any organisation, are not the type of people I would easily ask to spend time dining with. Yet we work together, vote on almost all the same issues, supposedly propound the same political objectives and campaign on the same party political platforms.

The reason being that my perception of them, as an individual, is not a particularly good one. It matters not only what the general public think of you (because of your public position) but also what your contemporaries think of you also.

There are politicians who will champion the cause of the poor, the oppressed and weak, yet in their political lives will lie, double-deal, back-stab and take every opportunity offered to further their own careers, no matter what it involves. To the general public they are doing what they proclaim, to their colleagues they are usually held in low esteem and certainly not trusted. Yet, they too would rise to their feet when Jim Wallis calls "Where are the prophets?" and they also would shout "We're here."

The question, therefore, remains, can someone be a prophet yet lack integrity? Let's be clear in the harsh world of politics, it's not a matter of being Mr. Nice-Guy; there are political battles to be fought and hard choices to be made, but for me it's about being open, frank and honest, even if that hurts or offends some people.

The only thing a politician has is his or her credible reputation. Once that has gone, once the trust disappears there is very little left. But if the public are not aware of the unpublished behaviour what does it matter, the reputation stays intact.

It all comes back to not pretending to be someone or something that you are not, otherwise you will soon get found out. For the believer that just doesn't refer to the general public; conscience and God's opinion are what differentiates those with integrity and those without.

TWELVE

In the Prologue I began with the events that led to a major disappointment for me, an outcome that wasn't an answer to prayer, not to my prayers anyway. But disappointments come and go, it's part and parcel of life and you realize that sometimes God says "No." I've already mentioned the fact that I failed to become leader of the EPLP but with hindsight it was a blessing in disguise. I can think of two other events where 'great' things could have been but were not to be. The first was connected to the European Court of Auditors, that august body, located in Luxembourg and having a Member of the Court from each member state (although what each finds to do now there are 25 of them, goodness only knows). Several hundred professional auditors actually do the work but the Court is responsible for the findings and publishes reports, including the annual report on the EU budget. Some members of the Court are politicians whilst others are career civil servants, either way it is an extremely well paid job with all the trimmings of your own 'cabinet' and chauffeur-driven car.

Jan Karlson, the affable Swedish President of the Court, who was a Social Democrat politician, came to my office in the Spring of 2001 to say that the British Member of the Court, John Wiggins, would be ending his mandate at the end of the year and that I should take his place. Great in theory, a million miles away from achievability. The UK had never appointed a politician to be a Member of the Court, the civil servants looked after their own and who was going to recommend me. Jan got the message and such was his wish to see me in Luxembourg that he must have done a few rounds chatting to people. As for me, I did nothing. Some time later the next thing I know the UK Ambassador to the EU, Nigel Schienwald is in my office asking if I had sent in my CV. Sent in my CV, for what? For the appointment of the UK member of the European Court of Auditors. HMG had asked the Secretary General of the European Parliament, the Council and the Commission to ask interested persons to submit their CVs by that coming Friday. It was now Tuesday. Oh and the British Civil Service had also been trawled.

I did a condensed CV, based solely on my work in Budgets and Budgetary Control in the Parliament, which looked pretty impressive, I thought.

Miraculously, I was then shortlisted and had to go to the Cabinet Office for an interview. There sat Sir John Kerr, Sir Stephen Wall (both former Ambassadors to the EU whom I knew and liked) and the Civil Service Commissioner (who he?). Sir John's first comment was something like "Terry, your CV isn't very long," to which my response was something like, "I didn't intend spending time doing a CV when this appointment is going to one of your own." Much spluttering and assurances that they were interviewing three people only and that the best man would get the job. It was stressed this was not a political appointment, meaning it wasn't the Prime Minister's recommendation, but that of the Head of the Civil Service who they would make the proposal to. This must have been stressed three times.

This had to be the most laid back interview I have every done; I was thoroughly enjoying myself, at one point after about 30 minutes, I said "You haven't asked me if I want the job, after all who wants to live in Luxembourg." I think it was at this point that my chances well and truly went. When Stephen Wall telephoned me the next day, he said that the Head of the Civil Service had not recommended my name to the Prime Minister. Hang on a minute, I thought the Prime Minister didn't have a say in it—I didn't say that but I certainly thought it. The person chosen was David Bostock, the civil servant whose name I had heard earmarked for the post even before Jan Karlson had come into my office.

The good news was Doris, my wife, didn't want me to get it, neither did the Secretariat of the Budget Committee or my colleagues in the Socialist Group. The fact that I didn't get it was no great loss.

The other 'great' thing that could have been and continues nicely this 'nearly man' saga was far more important.

I've always liked sports, played football, rugby, basketball, badminton and went swimming, and still run three times each week. And much as I can enjoy watching most sports my passion is for Rugby League and especially my home town team of Wigan whom I have supported from being a kid. I was, and still am, a minor (very minor) shareholder and know the directors reasonably well.

In the late nineties the Club had financial problems and all kinds of things were not going right. The Chairman and Vice Chairman had resigned and the club was left with only one director, Arthur Thomas, a really nice guy.

Doris and I were visiting friends in Boston, Massachusetts when on Saturday 25th October, 1997 I got a call from my office to ring Alan Rowley, urgently, the Commercial Manager at the club. The message said at any time, so I did. Unfortunately it was midnight in the UK and I woke up Alan's wife. He wasn't in but she said I needed to speak to Arthur Thomas and gave me his number.

I rang Arthur and the bottom line of the conversation was (and I paraphrase);

"We have financial backers, have a site for a new stadium, putting a financial package together to try and get the club out of debt. Would you like to be a director?"

As he said this, my eyes lit up, I looked at the telephone in disbelief, silently mouthed 'bloody hell' and felt like a kid who had just received his Christmas presents and birthday presents all on the same day. "Well Arthur," I replied as calmly as I could, "I'll have to see the business plan and the books of course, and we'll have to discuss it as soon as I get home." But, underneath I was saying, "Yes, yes, yes."

"Actually there's more to it, Terry," he went on. "We are floating the company on the stock exchange. This would give the shareholders real value and make them feel they had a real stake in the club.

"In that type of circumstance, we would normally have a banker as Chairman, but we thought it would be better to have someone whom the fans knew and trusted. So we wondered if you would like to be Chairman?"

I must have been ten feet in the air, silently shouting "Y—E—S—S—S."

I was walking the team out at Wembley Stadium already. Chairman of Wigan Rugby League Club, wow! "Well Arthur, I'm very flattered and of course if would be an honour but as I said, if we can discuss it when I get back next week" — (but yes, absolutely yes.)

Unfortunately, Arthur's plan was leaked to Dave Whelan the local millionaire who over that weekend bought out the two major shareholders for an extremely good price. So for three wonderful days I was going to be Chairman of the club of my passion, what more could you want.

When I did meet Arthur on my return, he had no recriminations about what had happened, "At least Dave will put money into the Club and ensure it survives which can only be a good thing." It wasn't quite what I was thinking but it turned out to be true.

So disappointments come and go, they are part of life's rich tapestry. Some things you would like, some things are opportunities for advancement, but what you never had, you can't miss. The ones that hurt or the ones that confuse are when you invest a lot of prayer and trust in God and he comes up with a different response. However, my disappointments in the Parliament are as nothing compared to Tony Hall or when Gill lost her babies or when Rebecca broke her neck or when Tunne Kelam was banished to his chicken farm or when Cedric was imprisoned and tortured. Life has to be put in perspective and it's no use asking Why? when things don't go as you would have wanted. Paul and Rebecca can proclaim God is good all the time and say, as St. Paul did, "We pray to have the strength to stick it out over the long haul."

Disappointments shouldn't discourage and the Christian politician will have many. Those who want to be the modern day prophets will find plenty of voices shouting them down.

If a society needs a soul then it needs good people to infuse it, time and time again, even after suffering disappointments and doubts.

Having just witnessed the 2004 United States Presidential election and seen the role that religion has overtly played in it, I could never imagine the same ever happening in any European country. Yet, as someone once said to me at one of our Prayer Breakfasts in Strasbourg, Christianity is the common thread that runs through Europe, you see it in laws, in cultures, in architecture, in art, in literature and in music. Every village in Europe has a church, many may now be empty but the legacy remains. When Jacques Delors set out to determine the Soul of Europe he knew that the EU was much more than an economic entity.

It is obvious from the interviews that in places of oppression people turn to the Church and when changes take place and affluent times arrive, God is forgotten. Although He isn't forgotten in those South African townships where they have liberty but no wealth. What is it about Western society that such a process can take place, except that is in the USA? Ulrich Miesel may be in a minority but he knows that it wasn't Marxism that was almighty and it's not capitalism that is almighty but only God is almighty and as he says, history will learn that lesson again. It's reflected by Tunne Kelam when he says that in rough times Christians can retain a quiet optimism for the future and that truth is the thing that makes you free.

The Baltic, South African and East German experiences make the same point that you can't separate the struggle for freedom and human rights from religion. They all talk about 'living in the truth' and 'the Spirit of the people not being crushed.' Compare that to the secular affluent world where so much is taken for granted and as long as we as individuals have our home comforts and our rights, then why should we bother about God, our neighbour or the ones the prophets cry out for.

Here's a quiz:

Name the five wealthiest people in the world.
Name five Nobel Prize Winners.
Name the last five 100 meters Olympic Gold Medal winners (men or women)
Name the last five F.A. Cup winners.
Name the last five best Actor/Actress Oscar Award winners.

Easy? Probably not but these are high profile people the best in their professions, who we read about on a regular basis. There are not second-raters but headline grabbers. However, they get forgotten with time, the applause dies, awards tarnish, achievements are forgotten, accolades and certificates are buried with their owners

Try another quiz:

Name the people who have taught you something worthwhile.
Name the people who have made you feel appreciated and special.
Name the teachers who helped you through school.
Name the people who you enjoy spending time with.
Name the friends who have helped you in a difficult time.

Far easier? Because these are the people who matter to you, who you set your standards by, who have given you emotions and feelings of worth. The people who make a difference in your life are not the ones with the most credentials, the most money or the most awards. They are the ones who care.

Ulrich Miesel, Boris Traikowski and their kind have left an impression on me, as has Cedric Mayson. Their stories are worth telling to show how God, working through ordinary people, can achieve extraordinary things which can have a lasting influence on many others.

★　★　★　★

In March 1993 on one of our regular visits to South Africa, Doris and I were taken by Cedric and his wife Penelope to Soweto University to hear the Imilonji Kantu choir. It was the 28th March and Doris's 50th Birthday. The auditorium was packed and we must have been the only white faces there. The choir, led by George Mxadane, sang at Nelson Mandela's inauguration and George's wife Mary used to work for the South African Council of Churches and became the President's P.A. They were knock-out. I had goose-pimples all over me as they sang and they have such an array of music.

The song I will always associate with the run up to the 1994 elections in South African is "From a Distance" sung by a variety of artists, my favourite being Bett Midler. It was played all the time, so when the compere, a dapper, middle-aged gentleman announced that Mary would sing it, the audience cheered like crazy. As she sang they were still excited but when she reached the line 'I just cannot comprehend what all this fighting's for', they just went wild, cheering and clapping to such an extent that she had to stop singing. On walks the compere, gesturing for them to sit down and keep quiet. The concert was a fund-raising event so people were running to the stage putting money on it, so chaos reigned.

When it was relatively calm the compere pleads for them to control themselves and let Mary sing the song through uninterrupted. *"You know,"* he said, *"You remind me of the father whose son had trained as a clergyman and was sent to his home village to be in charge of the church. The father was extremely proud, bursting with pride. On the Sunday as his son was preaching his sermon, half-way through the father stood up and shouted "Hallelujah." After the service the son took his father to one side and said, 'That was quite embarrassing for me.' He asked his father not to do it again, and in fact would buy him a new pair of shoes if he would not repeat what he did. So come the following Sunday, the son begins to preach. After about 20 minutes the father can restrain himself no longer and jumps to his feet and shouts 'Shoes or no shoes, Hallelujah!' Now you have the same feeling as the father, so please let her sing."* And they did. Then went wild.

In this life that we all have, a mere pin prick in time that we spend on this earth, there is so much to be thankful for that I want to shout, "Shoes or no shoes—Hallelujah" from the rooftops. I want to tell people to stop moaning and be grateful for what they have, but I don't because I don't want to offend them. (Would Ian Paisley care about offending them?) I want to constantly tell people that God is good, that He has poured out so many blessings on us that it fills me with absolute joy. But I don't unless it's in a pulpit, but never as a politician speaking to a secular audience. Were I an American, I wouldn't have a problem, but is that the way to do it?

There is Ibby with his commitment to God, praying as often as he can, living out his faith as instructed and realising that he is answerable to God for his actions at his life's end. He puts the likes of me to shame. I mentioned at the end of Chapter Seven that I have in my office a poster which reads "If you were arrested for being a Christian, would there be enough evidence to convict you?" I have to keep asking myself, "Well, would there?"

Most of the above chapter was written on the Eurostar train, as I travelled from Brussels to London and back after giving evidence at a House of Lords Committee on EU funding. We arrived back in Brussels as I wrote that last sentence above about the poster. An hour and a half later I was in the presence of a man who had been imprisoned and tortured because the evidence of his being a Christian was so overwhelming.

I meet a lot of people and many ask to see me, so on this occasion I left it to Olwyn, my then assistant in Brussels, to do my diary and trust that she can sort out whom I should see. I arrived in my office from the station and before long Peter Xu was walking in.

I had recently begun reading *The Heavenly Man*, a best seller in Christian bookshops, about a Chinese Christian called Brother Yun who suffered prolonged torture and imprisonment for his faith. Peter Xu (or Xu Yangzee) had been in prison with him. His story of what is happening in modern day China to Christians (and Muslims, which I knew of through my Amnesty contacts) was horrific as he described what he and his wife had endured. Yet there was no moaning, no misery; he could still thank God for all his blessings

173

and was a remarkably cheerful individual. His "Shoes or no shoes, Hallelujah" would make the rafters ring.

The really interesting thing of course is that the Christian church in China is expanding at a phenomenal rate despite the persecutions. Or as Peter Xu would say, because of the persecutions. If something is worth being persecuted for then it must be worth having. Because of his visit and because of the Amnesty contacts I tried to get a visit to China but the Embassy would not allow me to do a visit to meet with religious groups, or at least not the ones I was asking to meet. They would willingly help me to do a visit for cultural, economic, energy or whatever other reason but not for religious purposes. I declined. However, I want to watch this space, as Christians are persecuted in a variety of countries it hardly seems right to do nothing. One lady from North Korea whom I met, was imprisoned despite being a Party member, became a Christian in her prison camp and the horror stories she told would turn your stomach.

We in the West have no idea, can't even begin to imagine, what people like Peter Xu are going through every day. Why aren't the prophets of the West crying out about this, where is the Soul of Europe that should be reaching out to persecuted people everywhere?

I am extremely fortunate and blessed to have met and known so many good people, some mentioned in these pages, some mentioned in "Onward Christian Socialist" and countless others besides. The vast majority are not household names, quite the contrary they are everyday people who get touched by the Holy Spirit as they try to make this world a better place. And I suppose that should be the job of all politicians, especially those who are politicians with a real faith, or those who are motivated by their cultures, like Louise Ellman and Glenys Kinnock, which are rooted in faith.

Politics is about power, pure and simple. To get the power to change things, to make things better, to help the people you represent. But power can also corrupt. Remember what Maat Laar said in Chapter Three when he compared the power he had as Prime Minister to one of Tolkein's Rings, where it would be easy to exercise it for the wrong purposes. The European Parliament has a lot of power these days especially through the Budgets Committee. If you are a national MP and sitting on the opposition benches you have not so much as a little finger on the levers of power, but as an MEP everyone, who is prepared to make the effort can directly influence decisions and legislation.

In the mid-nineties, Andrew Marr, now the BBC political correspondent, was writing for the *Independent* newspaper. Sir Fred Catherwood, a Tory member but also a good colleague, had invited him to Strasbourg to assess the Parliament. I met with Andrew Marr and at the time I had just been the Rapporteur for the 1994 European Community Budget and was doing the 1995 one. His article when it appeared had the headline "Flynn Ran to Wynn, Now That's Power," and he wrote "Terry Wynn is probably the most powerful man in the European Parliament." Modesty went out of the window as I cut that out and stuck it on my wall for all to see.

In one little story about Commissioner Padraig Flynn having to come to my office to see me over a budgetary issue rather than me going to his office, Andrew Marr grasped how much budgetary power the Parliament had, especially over the Commission.

A more recent story I tell to emphasise power and not to make me anymore bigheaded than I already am concerns events following the war in Afghanistan when the international donor community were due to meet in Tokyo to pledge how much each would contribute to the re-building of Afghanistan.

I was at a basketball game in Ghent with the Belgian Finance Minister, whose team were playing. My mobile phone battery had run down so thankfully I wasn't receiving any calls to disturb me. When I arrived at my office the next morning my answer phone, and my now recharged mobile, were full of messages from Commissioner Schreyer, the Budgets Commissioner asking me to ring her urgently. So I did.

"Terry, Commissioner Chris Patten is on his way to Tokyo," she said, "And he wants to say that the EU will pledge a billion Euro over five years. But we have told him he can't say anything until I have spoken to you. We need to know it is okay."

Sounds good eh? What she really meant was, What will be the reaction of the Budgets Committee? But even so it demonstrates that same power.

The task is to turn that power that is given to politicians into giving Europe or individual nations a "Soul." A "Soul" that can echo the cries of the prophets for action against poverty, for help to the weak, to right the wrongs that affect so many people around this planet.

Politicians need guiding principles, ask Louise, ask Glenys; it's not merely a career, or something to do. The same guiding principles of the prophets (and in my case Jesus too) propelled by a belief that recognises that no man is God, nor is materialism; that this planet is put in our charge and it's our job to care for it and its peoples in a way that can glorify the maker of it.

It's bad enough being a politician and a Christian to advocate unpopular causes but I also advocate the case for nuclear energy with the same passion as I do the other two. As a shop steward from the nuclear industry once said to me some years ago, when I and only two other colleagues would see them on a visit to Brussels, "We have come to realise that there are no Brownie points in the Labour Party for supporting our industry, so thanks for coming." As a former power generating engineer and someone who cares deeply about the environment of this planet, I honestly believe that without Nuclear Power the future of this planet is in jeopardy. Wind, wave and solar power, which I encourage, will not meet future demands. If we want our kids and grandkids to have the same access to the things we take for granted (like simply switching on a light) then we need to acknowledge the role of nuclear power. After all you wouldn't want to be going for an operation and saying to the surgeon "Is the wind blowing today?"

There are still a billion people on this planet who have no access to electricity. Why should they not have their TV set, video recorder, air conditioning unit etc.? Energy is about to become THE big issue for the next decades, especially with the economic rise of India and China. As it was pointed out to me recently, if in the year 2030 every other family in India and China has one car then that will require 30% of the earth's energy resources. Who says politics and religion don't mix? This is after all God's planet and we are all His children.

When you love God, as with loving anyone, you will get hurt, it's a consequence of loving. Putting God's love into politics means the politician will face immense challenges. However, when your politics is driven by a solid faith and relationship with God, then the aim of putting a Soul into society becomes a cause.

"Meaningless, meaningless, all is meaningless," wrote the author of Ecclesiastes. Don't you believe it.

EPILOGUE

When I didn't become President of the European Parliament my intention was to plan a quick exit strategy. I couldn't resign immediately, that would be too much like sour grapes or 'taking my ball home', so I decided to give it a year maximum, and in that time begin to wind down and take things easy. My 15 years in the Parliament had been hectic and demanding, it was a 24/7 job (note the avante-garde terminology) but that was never a complaint when I enjoyed the work so much. So I was determined to ease back on the accelerator (or gas to any Americans reading this).

The Parliament operates through a committee system, there are 20 committees and normally a Member is appointed to two committees. Following the June 2004 elections, the European Parliamentary Labour Party was now down to 19 Members and there was no room for slackers or anyone trying to dodge their responsibilities on the committees.

I had said to Gary, the Leader of the EPLP, that if I failed to get the Presidency then I would take whatever was left in way of committee membership; in other words the ones that no-one else wanted I would take because I would be leaving within the year.

I was given the worst two, which no British Labour member wanted to be anywhere near. They were Agriculture and Budgetary Control.

The Agriculture Committee was full of pro-CAP members who would defend the Common Agriculture Policy at all costs. Thankfully, the Parliament doesn't have the final say on Agriculture, the Council of Ministers does. Which means that Parliament only gives opinions on the subject. Having come from the Budget Committee, with its all embracing power to this was, well, erm, different to say the least. However, I was the Chairman of a cross-party, multi-national grouping called LUFPIG (I know it sounds like a flying pig but it is the Land Use and Food Policy Intergroup, which has campaigned for reform of the CAP for years. So I knew the subject matter pretty well, the trouble being I was like a voice in the wilderness and Daniel in the Lion's Den at the same time. The frustration grew out of the inability to influence the committee in any way. Through LUFPIG we concentrated on influencing the Commission, where we were quite persuasive.

The Committee of Budgetary Control I had been a member of since 1989 and it was a good scrutiny committee. From 1999 to 2004 I didn't attend its meetings because of my being the Chairman of the Budgets Committee. Unfortunately, others did attend and it was hi-jacked by a variety of anti-Europeans who were prepared to use it for their own propaganda purposes. In that five years it had achieved for itself a pretty bad reputation within the Parliament and other members were not taking it seriously. That's why no-one wanted to go on it. So the idea was to try to get some sense into the Control Committee and my being there would give it some 'gravitas'. That was okay because I wouldn't fight to do any reports and I didn't have to do that much work, simply keep an overview of events. That's what I thought anyway until Paulo Casaca knocked on my door.

Paulo had been appointed the spokesman for the Socialist Group on the Control Committee; in Washington parlance the minority leader.

The most important report that the Committee does each year is that of analysing the European Court of Auditors annual report on the EU budget and then deciding whether to give 'discharge' to the Commission. I know discharge sounds like a medical condition but it's about discharging the Commission of its responsibilities. It's a lot of work and over the 15 years I had done three discharges (normally people do one). I really didn't want so much work and responsibility, knowing full well the time and effort that would be involved and the Discharge Report was the last thing I wanted.

Paulo had other ideas. "I'm not interested Paulo, give it to one of the many new, young members we have."

"They all want it but it needs someone with experience."

"Find someone else, what about Herbert?"

"Already committed to the anti fraud work."

"What about ...." There was nobody else. Paulo is very persuasive so I reluctantly accepted.

The work started in September 2004 and culminated with a vote in the Strasbourg Plenary the following April. It was a lot of work but the report was one of the best I'd ever done in all my time in the Parliament.

It made fundamental recommendations that will be acted upon by the Member States, the Commission and the Court of Auditors that can improve management and control systems and audit information to kill off once and for all the perception that the EU budget is riddled with incompetence and fraud. It gave me immense satisfaction and it was a report that needed to be done. In fact, it is probably my lasting legacy to the EU.

At about the same time that Paulo approached me, so did the Secretariat of the Budgets Committee. Parliament had created a temporary committee to analyse the EU budget to give it a position to negotiate with the Member States on the financing of the EU from 2007 to 2013. It was chaired by the new President of the Parliament but since he would really be a titular head and knew little about the EU Budget, I was asked if I could be the Vice President and in effect to do the work of the President.

I was tempted to say "get stuffed" but I didn't. I spoke to several people and eventually said yes. Another big task and another load of work which would run to the middle of 2005, then the negotiations would go on through to 2006 before there was a final deal.

Also, it was to be the UK Presidency of the EU from July 2005 for six months, then there would be a referendum in the UK on the Constitutional Treaty.

I decided to give it an extra year and leave in the middle of 2006. I'd be 60 years old then and that would be the deadline. It didn't go down well with Doris, my wife. Also, with there only being three Labour Members to cover the North West Region of England, I had taken on more areas of responsibility including the county of Cumbria which was half of the land area of the Region. In other words, instead of a winding down period, I found that I was busier than I have ever been.

Not getting the Presidency has allowed me to do worthwhile things within the House that will last for a long time and help the development of the EU.

But not being President has given me time at home which I would never have had if I had been successful at getting it. Especially with my family and grandson, James, with whom I have a real bond. But the best has been seeing David my son and Gill, his wife, having an addition to the family. After losing three babies, almost two years to the date of losing the first one when Doris received that telephone call at Heathrow Airport, Amelia Grace Wynn came into the world and I've had plenty of time to be with her. Something I would never have had as President. She is absolutely beautiful and a real gift from God.

I said in The Prologue that not getting the leadership of the EPLP was the best thing that happened to me. On reflection I can say the same thing about not being President of the European Parliament.